**What O**

My life motto is this: "If you want to be successful, read books written by people who are actually successful." That's Allan Blain. Finance and business success, sure, but Allan is a guy who has also found success in his personal life, spiritual life, and family life. So often I see finance books written by people who are broke and weight loss books written by people who are overweight! As a guy who knows Allan personally...he's the poster child of success.

—John Crist, Comedian, Author of the best selling book "Delete That"


This book is exhortation in the highest degree. It encourages the risk taking, God glorifying, faith walking life that Jesus calls us to. You'll leave with a recalibration of trials, success, and the adventure we were never called to stop living.

—Cody Hollister, NFL Wide Receiver, SuperBowl Champion

The truth may hurt, but the truth also sets you free. If you want a breakthrough, personally or professionally, this is the book you need. Allan Blain guides you through the storm and into newfound freedom.

—Dr. Kary Oberbrunner, CEO and WSJ and USA Today bestselling author of 13 books

Allan Blain's *Life's Hard Succeed Anyway* is an inspiration for anyone facing life's challenges. He opens up about personal stories that he's overcome, and shows you that success is about embracing adversity and perseverance. This book is a roadmap to triumph, a reminder that with resilience and determination, we can conquer any obstacle. A must-read for those seeking to thrive despite life's hardships.

—Zach Terrell, 2016 Western Michigan Quarterback and Academic Heisman Trophy Recipient

Allan and Nicole's enthusiasm for life is evident. This book is an extension of their mission to make the world a better place. The pages are filled with their life--lessons learned, heartbreaks, and triumphs. Allan bravely shares so people who want to reach their highest potential while navigating the ups and downs of life find success that only comes when you embrace it and take action.

—Joyce Martin Sanders, *The Martins*, 8 Dove Awards and 3 Grammy Nominations

I've had the privilege of being a small business owner for 44 years. Being the Patriarch of a large family, coupled with business trials, I know first hand that life can throw you curves. Allan Blain gives you a roadmap on how to navigate inescapable challenges in *Life's Hard Succeed Anyway.* Allan is transparent and raw for your benefit. Save yourself a great amount of heartache by applying Allan's first hand experiences to life's hard challenges and succeed anyway.

—Aaron Walker, Founder View From The Top

"Life's Hard Succeed Anyway" is an unfiltered dive into the reality of life's challenges. But rather than letting those challenges weigh you down, this book inspires a transformation of perspective. With its direct approach, it awakens the soul, urging readers to confront adversities head-on and morph them into stepping stones towards success. An essential read for anyone seeking a surge of motivation to persevere, regardless of the odds.

—Mike Kim, entrepreneur and Wall St. Journal and USA Today bestselling author of *You Are the Brand*

Life's Hard Succeed Anyway is a vulnerable, heartbreaking, yet inspiring story, written by an extraordinary human, filled with gems of practical wisdom to help you realize your true potential.

—Kendra Brassfield, Chief Executive Officer, Neolife International

Allan Blain's book, Life's Hard Succeed Anyway, leaves no room for excuses. Whether it's a career, dealing with your own personal struggles, or improving relationships, this book can help you achieve those goals. Whatever we want to achieve in life takes perseverance, persistence, and a strong desire to never give up. Allan's book gives the reader the tools needed to succeed, and the motivation to do it. No matter where you are today, this book will challenge you to get to where you want to be tomorrow.

—Victoria Robinson, Author and CEO &
Founder of Reassemblelife.com

Allan Blain has been an entrepreneur that I've known for almost a decade and he's more than qualified to write this book. I've witnessed him go through personal challenges and obstacles in his journey to success; including him having to cancel an event due to his troubled past. Anyone who reads this book will benefit greatly from Allan's life experiences and lessons.

—Simon Chan, CEO and Founder of MLM Nation

A must-read playbook for aspiring leaders who are tired of watching their life from the sidelines and who want to step into the game to achieve what they were meant to become. Don't settle for an average life filled with regrets, stalled out from highlight reels of hurts from your past. You don't have to drift at sea, or even tread water. Allan provides a roadmap for the person who wants to embrace their true identity and step into an abundant, purpose-driven life.

—Derek Champagne,
Best Selling Author of Don't Buy A Duck

Life's Hard Succeed Anyway is such an easy and enjoyable read, I couldn't put it down and finished it in one sitting. Allan's story of adversity and success are proof that circumstances don't make or break you, they reveal you. I love the insight, encouragement, transparency, and hope this book delivers.

—Dwight Johnson, Founder & CEO
Bend Soap Company

Life hits us all hard and doesn't stop. The torrents and the waves keep coming. Though I know Allan and Nicole, until I read this book I had no idea all of the trauma and obstacles they have faced along the way. From sibling suicides, to job loss, financial ruin, health issues, and on and on - many stacked atop one on another at the same time—so much so that most would have justified chronic bitterness, anger, despair, hopelessness, and rage.

They instead focused on gratitude, forgiveness, and faith in a God who loves us and wants the very best for us. This is a story of amazing renewal and restoration with an undying and confident hope in the midst of heartbreaking devastation. What an inspiration! What amazing hope and faith! I encourage you to read this book and rejoice in the renewal of your faith in the God who truly cares for you.

—Omar Hamada, MD, MBA and Former LTC
US Army Special Forces.

This book is a must read if you're ready to turn your setbacks into a setup for greater success. Everyone will relate with aspects of Allan's story regardless of the hardships they're facing! He's not just relatable though, he shares the lessons he's learned along with a proven path forward so that we too can succeed in spite of life's painful hardships.

—Josh Clark, Entrepreneur, Former GA State
Representative, and US Senate Candidate

Allan Blain filled Life's Hard Succeed Anyway with exciting encouragement to help motivate us to have more independence and structure. Allan finds a way to capture his audience with life lessons and practical steps for leveling up regardless of your goals. We highly recommend Allan's relatable message especially if you're feeling a little complacent and need a motivational bump.

—Brandon & Jordyn Clark,
CoFounders of Studio 1:9

Life hitting you like a ton of bricks? Big challenges feel overwhelming? Ready for your breakthrough? *Life's Hard Succeed Anyway* will provide truth, hope, and a plan of action for overcoming your hard.

—Chad Johnson, Entrepreneur,
Author & Coach to High Achievers

# LIFE'S HARD SUCCEED ANYWAY

## STOP SETTLING AND SEIZE THE LIFE YOU WERE CREATED FOR

## Allan Blain

ethos
collective

Published by Ethos Collective
Powell, Ohio
EthosCollective.vip

LCCN: 2023914066
Paperback ISBN: 978-1-63680-200-8
Hardcover ISBN: 978-1-63680-201-5
Ebook ISBN: 978-1-63680-199-5

# A Special Thank You to My Wife

To my wife, Nicole, who has journeyed with me through
thirty-one years of marriage and counting,
the births of our six blessings from the Lord,
twenty-two moves across four states,
multiple career changes, and
more challenges and adversity than we can count.
You have stood prayerfully and faithfully by my side
and have been my biggest cheerleader
not only through the good times,
but also in the lowest of lows.
I have always been able to depend on your support.
Never, for even a moment, did I feel alone.
Your selflessness, unwavering devotion, and continual
encouragement
have always been a catalyst to everything I do,
and this book is no exception.
You are a phenomenal example of a Proverbs 31 woman.
Thank you for being my trusted best friend,
my soulmate, the love of my life,
and for sticking with me when life got hard,
so we could succeed anyway.

# CONTENTS

# FOREWORD

I thought my education ended with a college degree, but it was just beginning. I was about to be enrolled in the school of hard knocks after I was rear-ended by an 18-wheeler while coming home from work. As a result of back and neck pain, I took pain meds given to me by a doctor to cope with my injuries. Within three months, I was addicted to pharmaceutical drugs. My story is not uncommon today. Many become addicts because of a sports injury or car accident. Some of you can relate.

I've learned that everything in life comes with a price tag. Success is no exception. As a new minister, I had the unrealistic expectation that working for the Lord would be full of pleasures without pain. The joy of serving God is without question an honor; however, it hasn't come without a cost. The greatest lessons from the highs and lows of ministry were learned outside the classroom. I wouldn't trade my eight years of seminary training for anything, but the most profound spiritual formation came from loss and suffering rather than classroom learning.

Life offers no shortcuts to spiritual growth. It's a principle realized in all walks of life. Codfish is a lucrative business in the Northeast. Distribution of the fish posed a problem to the sellers though. Freezing the fish before shipping seemed like the logical step for transportation.

However, the flavor was compromised in the process. Next, they experimented with shipping the fish in large tanks of seawater to keep them alive. This didn't work either. Not only was the process more expensive, but it also proved to be worse because the meat became mushy. The solution was to ship the fish in a tank of water with their natural enemy, the catfish.

Throughout the trip from the East to the West Coast, the irritable catfish pestered the codfish.

When they arrived, the cod retained its flavor and texture as if they had just been caught from the sea.

Every one of us is in a tank of inescapable circumstances. Each day, we face God-appointed "catfish" that bring specific pressure to shape us into the image of Christ. Understanding how the economy of God worked changed my perspective.

Suffering and struggle intersect with God's sovereignty. They are God's divine instruments for personal growth.

Credibility is not received, it's earned through the crucible of hard work, struggles, and sweat equity. While Allan Blain has not arrived, he's been on the journey a long time, and for that, I want to glean from him. He understands that our direction is more important than our destination. He's a man who can savor the sweet because he's tasted the sour.

Life's Hard Succeed Anyway is a motto we all should live by. Whether it's unexpected financial struggles, battles with sickness, a surprising diagnosis from a doctor, or the sudden loss of a loved one or a close friend, circumstances can cause us to grow weary. It would be helpful if emails arrived every Monday at 8:00 a.m. with the memo, "In a month you're going to deal with this trial, so go ahead and put it on the calendar to prepare." Unfortunately, that's not how life works. Adversity will either build us up or tear us down. It is through life's challenges that we find out what we're really made of. When God tests a man or woman in Scripture, it is never to break them down. It's meant to build them up.

In his book, Allan shares his personal life experiences. From nearly drowning while surfing at Morro Bay to health struggles with his wife, Nicole, to a cancer diagnosis for one of his daughters, he is the father, husband, and business leader he is today because of adversity. The book walks the reader through practical insights learned through the crucible of trials or the waves of life, as Allan calls them.

He comments, "As we navigated all those storms, I began to see that while I can't avoid the waves, I can prepare for them. In fact, I discovered that waves have the potential to propel me to something bigger. Each time we enter a wave, we can learn how to ride the next one a bit better. After years of looking for peaceful waters, I eventually learned the truth—in Christ we can have peace and joy even in the middle of the storm."

This book is raw and real. It's also challenging and encouraging. He points us to the only hope we have for enduring on earth: Jesus Christ. Jesus lived a life we couldn't, died a death we should have, and rose from the grave on the third day to give anyone who professes faith in him assurance for eternal life tomorrow. But the free gift of salvation is more than a one-way ticket to heaven after we die. He empowers us with the Holy Spirit to overcome any situation we face today. The only failure in life is when we fail to learn from our failures. Every mistake is an opportunity to learn. School is always in session, and graduation is unattainable in this life.

Life's Hard, Succeed Anyway is a field guide for navigating whatever life throws at you. Don't just read it. Put the principles into practice.

Robby Gallaty, PhD
Pastor, Long Hollow Church
Author, *Growing Up and Recovered: How An Accident, Alcohol, and Addiction Led Me To God*

# BECAUSE LIFE'S HARD

Have you ever felt like your unique challenges get in the way of enjoying success in a particular area of your life? Challenges that hold you back from business, financial, physical, or relational success, stealing your time and keeping you from becoming the person you know you can be. That's certainly how I've felt in the past. If life keeps you from being a present parent, has knocked you down spiritually, physically or financially, or you feel like you're failing in any other way, "Life's Hard Succeed Anyway" is going to be music to your ears, breath for your soul and an asset for your life.

During the fifty-one years I have lived so far, I've endured many of those challenges. I even allowed some of them to hinder me from living my best life for a season. Thankfully, I refused to remain a victim of circumstances and poor choices.

I have walked through some deep dark valleys. I've lost loved ones too young, lived on welfare, and struggled with alcohol. Whether you're in a corporate board room or a county jail, I can relate. My life has been touched by death, divorce, cancer and more.

I've learned that challenges will always exist. I expect my next fifty-one years will see plenty more tough things–though, I trust fewer will be of my own doing. Each of us is in one of three seasons. We either just came through a challenge, we are in the middle of one, or we are approaching the next one.

Challenges are like waves in the sea. They keep coming regardless of the weather or the date on the calendar. And though we know the waves are coming, there's no way to know how big each one will be or how often they will appear. Some seasons feel like tidal waves–the next one forms before the last one has passed. Other seasons bring waves that merely lap on the shore–the sea looks calm ahead. Regardless of the season you are in, I'm confident this book will equip you to overcome and develop a life's hard succeed anyway mindset.

I'll never forget being on a podcast with my good friend Simon Chan. I shared a few of the hard things my family has been through. He told me that one of his mentors had described a swap meet. Everyone laid all their life challenges out on display. You could examine all the other tables and trade challenges with anyone of your choosing. His mentor told him that after looking at everyone else's challenges, you'd gladly choose to keep your own. I love that perspective. It helps me keep a victor rather than a victim mindset.

In the next pages I tell my story as well as the lessons I've learned because I know life's hard, and my greatest desire is to help you succeed anyway.

# LIFE'S (NOT) A BEACH

*Everything is hard until it gets easy.*
*At one point it was hard for each of us to*
*chew solid food, walk or even talk.*
*We must be willing to be bad at something long*
*enough to get good at it.*

When you plan a trip to the ocean, you may picture soft sandy shorelines covered with colorful towels, blankets, and beach umbrellas. Braver beachcombers may imagine magnificent waves swelling to heights only seen on Pacific islands. On a picture-perfect beach day, sailboats and yachts line the horizon until a cloudless sky gives way to the most vibrant sunset you've ever experienced.

Wouldn't it be wonderful if life looked like a postcard seashore? Unfortunately, life is not a Bali beach. No, life seems more like the rocky banks of California's central coast.

Situated between Los Angeles and San Francisco, Morro Bay is best known for Morro Rock, the huge volcanic mound situated at the end of the beach.

Morro Rock, the site of my near death college surfing experience, on a day when the waves were breaking near the top of the smaller rock pictured on the right.

Surf guides call the waves at Morro Rock dependable. Novice surfers see the beautiful waves without understanding all that those crests and swells mean. During my college years, I was one of those less skilled surfers.

The waves looked phenomenal as I drove by Morro beach on my way to church that Sunday morning. My buddy and I made plans to return there after service. He had his boogie board, and

I planned to surf. We had the entire beach to ourselves. Honestly, an empty beach on a Sunday afternoon should have been my first clue.

My second mistake came in the form of my wetsuit. The one I owned, from my water skiing days, zipped in the front and I had left it at home. Surf suits zip in the back in order to avoid laying on that zipper as you paddle out to the waves. Unfamiliar with all the Velcro and safety attachments of the back-zip suit I borrowed from my friend, I put on the gear but didn't get everything secured properly—something I wouldn't know until later.

Paddling out, a few hundred yards past the massive breaks was a bear, but our excitement swelled. Those waves looked exhilarating— "blown out" but more than double overhead in size—we both thought the day promised to be amazing. The majesty of what many call the Gibraltar of the Pacific loomed nearby, and after a lengthy struggle to arrive outside the breakers, my buddy caught one and successfully rode his boogie board to the shore.

He was long gone when I attempted to catch my first swell. However, before I could even get situated on the board, the water picked me up and pounded me under. It felt like I had been punched in the back and then put inside a spinning front load washing machine. The unsecured zipper opened down my back and my wetsuit filled up like a water balloon. When the turbulent spinning subsided, I started paddling with all my might.

I had learned just enough about surfing to know I needed to blow bubbles to find out which way was up after being tossed around like a rag doll. At least twenty-feet down, I headed in the direction of the bubbles.

I knew that I should be able to see myself getting closer to the surface because the water gets lighter as you move closer to the sun. On that day, although I was confident I was heading in the right direction, the water grew darker and darker. Running out of air and fighting for my life, I pushed myself as hard as I could.

Despite the message of the water color, I kept striving in the direction of the bubbles. To this day, I can't tell you for certain how far under that wave had taken me. But I do remember thinking, *This is it. My life is over.* And I distinctly recall two clear thoughts. *There is so much I will never accomplish. I am not going to get to say goodbye to mom.* No matter how hard I swam, the color of the water grew darker and I sank deeper and deeper. I was quickly running out of air. No one knew I was there. No one was coming to help me. *This is my*

*life. I wasted it. I didn't get to use my life for any-*
*thing meaningful. Nineteen years for nothing.*

That peace everyone talks about just before you drown overwhelmed me. I eventually stopped fighting, closed my eyes and let go of life.

I don't know whether I passed out, fell asleep, or died. I'm not even sure how much time passed between my last thought and being startled by my foot touching the ocean floor.

Somehow, I had drifted down far enough that my feet reached sand. A moment of hope overpowered my exhaustion. Drained to my limits, I gave all I had and pushed off. My water balloon wetsuit and the insignificant inertia of my feet against the sand didn't seem too promising, and everything moved in slow motion as I lost consciousness again.

The next thing I remember was a gasp for air that jerked me back to reality. Some have told me the board must have pulled me to the top because it was attached by a leash to my ankle. But the fact I came up headfirst rather than feet first leaves some doubt about that theory. I often wonder if God sent an angel to drag me from the depths because it doesn't seem likely that my extremely feeble push off the depths of the ocean floor could have propelled me all the way to the surface with a wetsuit still full of water.

I was blessed to suffer no lasting effects from my bad decision and have since realized that my Sunday surfing expedition provides a great life metaphor.

I wanted to go surfing that day despite the fact I couldn't handle the waves. I saw adventure ahead, but I didn't bother to recognize that even the most experienced surfers that had lined the coastline off that volcanic mound earlier that morning as I drove to church had avoided the waters on that particular afternoon.

I learned a valuable lesson at Morro Rock that day. Going forward, I recognized my limits and paid attention to the more seasoned surfers. If only more people would learn a similar lesson and apply it to life.

Much of the world has ignored the warning signs and followed their desire to ride the biggest of life's waves before they are adequately equipped. They ignore the advice of those who've learned the hard lessons. Don't let that be you. Use the content contained in this book, my failures, hardships and lessons I learned to warn, equip and inspire you to ride the waves of life successfully.

Currently, the average person is drowning in $20,000 of debt, and when you add mortgages to the mix, that number increases to more than

$100,000 per person. [1]The search for bigger and better has resulted in too many people getting pulled into addiction and destructive behavior. They think numbing agents like drugs, alcohol, burying themselves in busyness, and other addictions can help them avoid the crashing waves. But they don't. The JAMA network reported an estimated one in every eight adult deaths from 2015 to 2019 could be attributed to alcohol use. [2]

While we'd prefer to pretend only those who live the most reprehensible kinds of lives get wiped out, most of us know the opposite is true. The beautiful swells and troughs we paint by over-spending, chasing perfection, and numbing our problems with ineffective options are quite deceiving. I know firsthand.

Too many people have grown so accustomed to the pounding waves, they don't even try to get out. They know what they're experiencing isn't pleasant, but the most they do is switch out surfboards. It's like putting a frog in a pot of cool water and turning up the heat. As long as the discomfort

---

[1]    Fay, Bill. *Debt.org* "Key Figures Behind America's Consumer Debt. Updated April 3, 2023 https://www.debt.org/faqs/americans-in-debt.

[2]    Esser, Marissa B., PhD, Sherk, Adam, PhD, Leung, Gregory, PhD, et al. *JAMA Network.* "Estimated Deaths Attributable to Excessive Alcohol Use Among US Adults Aged 20 to 64 Years, 2015 to 2019". November 1, 2022. https://jamanetwork.com/journals/jamanetworkopen/fullarticle/2798004

comes gradually, the frog will stay right there until what started as a pleasant bath eventually takes his life.

Unfortunately, I can relate. At one time, from the outside, my life looked like a sunny coastline. However, on the inside, each day felt more like the cold waves from Morro Rock pummeling me into a rocky shore. Every time one swell would subside, another would hit me hard, and try as I might, I couldn't escape. I moved my family twenty-two times in thirty years in an attempt to find smooth water, but depression, cancer, alcohol addiction, family tragedy, and more caught up with me every time. Like the frog in the pot, we found ourselves so acclimated to the problems, we just trudged through. We quit trying to catch the wave and let the water pull us under and carry us as it pleased.

Maybe you are where I was not that many years ago. You feel as though you are capable of more, like you are equipped to play much bigger. You desire to make a greater impact and leave a larger legacy. Something inside is calling you to grow more, become more, and accomplish more, but you feel like you lack something. Let me help you uncover what is lacking.

It's been said that a life not evaluated is a life not worth living. My goal is to show you how to get you off the sidelines and enter this exciting game called life. I want this book to help you to toss aside complacency, stop settling, craft a compelling life vision, punch fear in the face, and start succeeding in life's most important areas–spiritually, relationally, personally, professionally and financially.

I've ridden enough waves of life to develop tools to equip you to live the life you were created for. In the following pages, you'll find out how to clarify your vision, so you can see where you are going, gain clarity about why you are heading there, and ensure you are journeying with the right tribe. I will share the ways I've changed my mindsets and perspectives as well as some practical strategies I've discovered that have helped me win despite the challenges that continue to come. The storms of life don't need to cause you to lose your way. They have the potential to become the catalyst to build the character, capabilities, and confidence that allow you to seize the life you were created for and succeed anyway.

## Life Is Not a Highlight Reel

Few realize it, but a lot of the turmoil in life is self-inflicted. Trying to live above our means, staying in lackluster careers, and living without purpose has created a canvas of discontent, divorce rates, addictions and more. My friend got a new car; I think I might need a new car. Never mind the fact that my friend has been saving for years to buy it. The neighbor and his wife seem so much happier since they went to Europe; maybe we should plan a trip. No one realizes some of these folks rarely even talk to each other inside their home and certainly don't feel heard, understood, known or appreciated.

The practice is as old as the earth; however, social media made it even worse. Beach scenes, new hairstyles, beautiful cakes, fancy clothes, perfect gardens. And in between each post we see an ad for our latest craving because our phone has learned to eavesdrop.

A quick Google search will give you countless funny comparisons between Instagram and reality. But as much as we can easily see through the lack of reality and may chuckle at the airbrushed beauties and photoshopped puppies shown next to their real counterparts, we should be equally heartbroken for the people who believe those glamourous highlights are real.

Counselors and psychologists agree that social media highlight reels have the greatest negative impact on teens and young adults. Underdeveloped brains don't understand the crests and troughs of life, so it's easy for them to compare themselves to what pops up online. They don't see the hours the bodybuilder or fitness model puts in at the gym before he or she posts their last lift session or the overtime their friend's dad worked for five years to take his family on that cruise. Social media can make everything look easy.

Even adults fall into the trap of comparisons. Camera filters subtract years and remove wrinkles just as easily as they can make a teen look like a prom queen. Plus, too much time focusing on the lives of others can alter the way the feel-good chemicals in our brains react, distracting people from important real-life relationships and problems. [3]

But what if you could find a way to overcome the attraction of the highlight reels and reality television? When I discovered my true identity, I found I didn't need those comparisons. By adjusting my mindset, I began to see a way forward to success.

---

[3]   Mally, Clint and Flethcher, Sarah LPC, LAC. *Sandstone Care* "Social Media Effects On Teens: 8 Things You Didn't Know About Social Media And Your Teen's Mental Health." Updated October 27, 2022. https://www.sandstonecare.com/blog/social-media-effects-on-teens-8-things-you-didnt-know-about-social-media-and-your-teens-mental-health/

# People are in Pain

The only things more popular than the highlight reels of social media are the YouTube blooper videos and reality television. Why? Because if we can't live up to the image of the prom queen, we can at least commiserate with the guy who very unsuccessfully tried to ride his skateboard down the railing.

We've come to a place in our culture where pain causes laughter or at least intrigue. Much of what we watch on America's Funniest Home Videos and YouTube clips involves someone hurting themselves in a less than intelligent fashion, and Hollywood strands people on mountains and deserts, or puts a group of people in a house together to see who can last the longest in an agonizing environment. All the while, television ratings rise while the world watches the back-biting misery. We've become a society of people watchers looking for the elusive perfect beach while often settling for the fact that our pain isn't as great as those on the screen.

Whether you enjoy playing in the water or sitting on the shore, nearly everyone eventually hopes for a beach umbrella or cabana with a lounge and a cool drink. We may intend to simply rest, nonetheless, if we're not careful settling into that cozy position can become painful. The sun moves, and we lose the shade, the tide comes in, or a storm blows through taking our shelter with it. If we happen to get too comfortable and perhaps fall asleep, what started as a lovely afternoon on the beach will end with a horrific sunburn or worse.

But don't we do the same thing in life?

We stop dreaming, start settling, and accept living a life of quiet desperation. Simply going through the motions with no real plan, no life giving dreams, and no clear and compelling vision is a sad state of affairs and I believe a big reason why so many are unable to successfully weather life's storms.

> PEOPLE WILL CHANGE WHEN THE PAIN OF STAYING THE SAME IS WORSE THAN THE PAIN IT TAKES TO CHANGE.
>
> "JILLIAN MICHEALS

It's like the story of the howling dog. An old man sits on a porch with his pooch that howls non-stop. After hours of the incessantly painful noise, the neighbor finally goes over to investigate.

"What's up with your dog making all the noise? He sounds like he's in pain." he asks the old man.

"He's been laying on a nail all day," the old man replies.

The neighbor is now doubly confused. "Why doesn't he just move?"

"He eventually will. He does this everyday. It just doesn't hurt enough yet. When the pain gets bad enough, he will move."

And so goes the world.

Far too many go through the motions of living in quiet desperation. They share their complaints, but the person listening often has a sadder story to tell. The pain stories turn into a game of one-upmanship. In fact, if we let ourselves get dragged in, we might even begin bragging about the pain, subconsciously willing it to get worse so we have a better story to tell. The more pain we endure, the more we get used to it, and rather than get off the nail, we just keep howling.

## The Cost of Settling

You may think you'd never be that dog and just put up with the pain; however, avoidance can be just as deadly. Every day a large percentage of the population misses out on an adventurous life because they want to avoid the pain. People stay in mediocre careers and refuse to take a chance on themselves. Playing it safe feeds the allusion of a pain free existence, but have you considered the cost?

The teen who fears the wild rides at the amusement park misses the excitement if she never tries them. Conflict makes the story interesting. What would Raiders of the Lost Ark be without the rolling boulders and great truck chase? Can you imagine the Toy Story series without the mean kid next door, Star Wars without Darth Vader and Anakin Skywalker, or Top Gun without Maverick's nemesis Iceman?

Even real-life heroes are born out of adversity. No one would have known about Captain Sully, the 57 year old pilot of the 150 passenger Airbus A320, if the engine hadn't failed on January 15, 2009 forcing him to land on the Hudson River. And though now she has millions of followers as well as a movie featuring her story, most outside her community would never have heard of Bethany Hamilton if she had played it safe and not gotten back on that surfboard after losing her left arm in a shark attack at age 13.

Many amazing pilots fly daily, but without some sort of calamity, the reach of their impact is limited. Likewise, numerous folks unknown to society have survived shark attacks, but few have turned their mishap into a platform to impact the world around them. Heroes know that the hard times are coming, prepare for them, and use them to fuel their future rather than define their past. Rather than remaining a victim, they become an overcomer.

> WE NEVER PASS THROUGH A STORM OF LIFE AND REMAIN THE SAME. WE ARE ALWAYS CHANGED BY IT. THAT'S THE PURPOSE IN THE PAIN. LOOK UP AND LET IT GROW YOU, NOT DESTROY YOU.

Life is hard for everyone. Fortunately, we can choose which hard we face. Being fit and healthy takes dedication and discipline. It is hard. However, being overweight, unhealthy, sick and tired can be even harder. Being relationally rich takes time, energy and sacrifice. But a shallow and unfulfilling relationship is painful. Financial success requires hard work and time. The alternative is being broke without options. Which hard will you choose?

I know what it's like to choose that life of settling. I did it for a season. For years, I let the familiar drive my career choices. My entire family suffered until the "nail" became so painful it affected them too. Complacency is just as hard as working toward a vision; I feel like I've moved from a lifeboat to a yacht, and I want to help you get there too.

# Build Your Ark Before it Rains

Many search for the sunny shores of Lake Perfect, as I did for far too many years, but the truth is the only thing guaranteed in this life are waves. Even Morro Rock, a shoreline that boasts a dependable surf, offers consistent clean waves only thirty percent of the time and light beginner style waves make up less than ten percent of the surf.[4] More often than not, the waves at Morro can't be conquered.

The same is true of life. You can't stop the crashing deadly waves, but you can be ready for them. In his song, "Build a Boat," Colton Dixon sings, "I know Your rain is coming . . . I'll build a boat so let it rain." And that's what we have to do to survive the turbulent waters of life. How do you think those crews survive the treacherous waters of the Bering Sea during crab season? They have boats big enough to withstand the thirty-foot swells that crash onto the deck and turn to ice.

Though smaller than modern cruise ships, Noah's five hundred ten foot long boat withstood forty days of storms and another few hundred days of waves crashing into it. When God told the five-hundred-year-old man rain would fall and floods

---

[4]    *Surf-Forecast.* accessed June 9, 2023. https://www.surf-forecast.com/breaks/Morro-Rock

would cover the Earth, Noah listened and began to build a boat.

In order to be ready for the inevitable waves, we need to build our ark before the rains start to fall. If Noah had waited for the first drop before he believed the promise of precipitation, we wouldn't have survived. Likewise, if you wait until trouble hits, the waves have the potential to knock you down, pull you under, and carry you off.

Through the years, my wife and I have learned to better prepare for and "read" the waves of life. We've discovered much better ways to ride them out and have built a seaworthy boat that God uses to protect us when they get too big to handle.

We view the challenges of life so much differently now than in our earlier years, and believe they are, as my good friend Pastor Robby Gallaty says, "the master's degree of character development." The apostle Paul agreed.

*We can rejoice, too, when we run into problems and trials, for we know that they help us develop endurance. And endurance develops strength of character.... Romans 5:3-4 (NLT)*

Nicole, my bride since 1992, and I have had some hard waves crash on us over the past couple of decades, and we want to use the lessons learned and the comfort that God has given us to encourage, equip and comfort others. Before I get into some practical application contained in this book, I'd feel negligent in my duties and calling if I failed to share with you that we've found that the ultimate source of our strength, hope, and success comes from the Lord Jesus Christ, our identity as His children, and acknowledging that we can do nothing of substantial greatness apart from him. He provides air for our lungs, causes our hearts to beat, our minds to work well, and so much more. We are so grateful to know that God doesn't just use the smartest, most talented or most perfect people. If He did, we both would have been long overlooked. Rather, He looks for the humble and those willing to allow their lives to be used to bring Him glory and honor so that nobody can boast in themselves.

> *Brothers and sisters, consider your calling: Not many were wise from a human perspective, not many powerful, not many of noble birth. Instead, **God has chosen what is foolish in the world** to shame the wise, and **God has chosen what is weak in the world** to shame the strong. **God has chosen what is insignificant** and despised in the world —what is viewed as nothing—to bring to nothing what is viewed as something,*

*so that no one may boast in his presence*. - 1 Corinthians 1:26-29 (CSB)

One of the greatest things God has used to comfort us has been others—groups of like-minded individuals, people who understand the waves of life are coming and want to help us navigate the waters. We want to pass along that gift of friendship and mentoring we've been given, so we've created an online community. We understand that isolation is the enemy of excellence so we invite you to join us now, even as you continue to read, at our free online *Succeed Anyway Community*. Simply email support@AllanBlain.com and include the words "Succeed Anyway Community" in the subject line or scan this QR code.

You will find a like-minded community to assist you in maximizing success in your faith, family, fitness and finances. A place where you can network, ask questions, collaborate, and be supported as you stop settling, craft a compelling vision, and seize the life you were created for.

I don't know what kind of wave might be crashing in on you right now. Perhaps you've come through the unthinkable. And none of us know the storms that lie ahead. Maybe you feel like your friends and family can't relate, don't understand, or just don't care about your situation in general.

> CHALLENGES (ADVERSITIES OR DIFFICULTIES) SHOULD NOT DEFINE US, BUT RATHER REFINE US.

Nicole and I have had our fair share of hardships. And even if we haven't experienced exactly what you're going through, we can certainly empathize with various struggles and challenges. If you could hear me tell my story, I believe you would hear my heart and see the genuine care in my eyes when I tell you that I sincerely want to help. It's my purpose for writing this book. In fact, in order to assist you in dealing with challenges, I've created an Adversity Assessment. Much like blood work gives you a head start on discovering health problems, this assessment can reveal your ability to handle adversity. I can help you see how resilient you are when you have to pass through future challenges. Find out now by scanning that QR code or visit AllanBlain.com/aa to take the free three-minute assessment.

Even more encouraging, I know the one who has felt every emotion, every temptation, every pain. Jesus Christ is really most capable to be there for you in the midst of your storm, just as he has been for us, and everyone else that has been willing to turn their eyes towards him and put their hope in him. My heart's desire is that the pages that follow will be a comfort and a resource with some practical application to help you win. (All free resources contained in this book can be located at AllanBlain.com/lhsa).

# PART ONE

# TREADING WATER

*Failure is not a bad thing.*
*It's a necessary part of learning,*
*growing and improving.*

# CHAPTER ONE
# WHEN LIFE HITS YOU

I 've never heard anyone say, "I hope life punches me in the face." Still, people wake up every day and walk into situations that invite just that. It's like the commercial from the 1980's "No one says I want to be a junkie when I grow up." Yet, more than forty-one million Americans needed treatment for a drug use disorder in 2020. [5] I walked right into life's punches several times before I found my purpose and took hold of my life. It may have started with my rough relationship with my dad or when I gave up on my dreams.

---

[5] *The White House,* April 21, 2022. https://www.whitehouse.gov/briefing-room/statements-releases/2022/04/21/fact-sheet-white-house-releases-2022-national-drug-control-strategy-that-outlines-comprehensive-path-forward-to-address-addiction-and-the-overdose-epidemic/

# Childhood Dreams

Little ones everywhere dream of being ballerinas, firefighters, doctors, nurses, or mermaids. Grown-ups feed their imaginations with phrases like, "You can be anything you want to be when you grow up."

But the encouraging words turn sour during those late middle school/high school years. The ballerinas and pianists are told that they can't make a living in the arts. Parents, teachers, and counselors begin coaching kids to pick safe, reliable careers. Even if the teen forges ahead with a bigger vision, adults tell them they need a back-up plan, and a host of eighteen-year-olds register for college with no idea what they will do with a degree if they finish the four years.

I had dreams. Major League Baseball had been on my radar since the family lifted the ban on sports when I was eleven. Prior to that, we attended a church with a lot of rules. We couldn't play sports or celebrate holidays. I spent time in the principal's office during holidays such as Christmas, Valentine's Day and Easter because I wasn't allowed to color the hearts, cupids, Easter bunnies, or Christmas trees with the rest of my class during those seasons in elementary school. After we changed churches, the world of sports opened, and I participated full force. I was on the high school football, basketball, and baseball teams, and I will admit I was pretty good.

During my freshman, sophomore and junior football seasons, I was the quarterback. My senior year, my brother joined the varsity team as a sophomore and took my spot, moving me to cornerback. It was a real blow to my ego. Fortunately, I still had baseball.

Baseball consumed my senior year of high school and freshman year of college. I thought I was headed for the big leagues. But shortly after my accident at Morro Rock, I met a girl—a girl I loved more than baseball. Nicole and I had a whirlwind relationship. We met at nineteen and within 6 months, to the shock of our parents, got engaged. Six months later, five days after Nicole's twentieth birthday, we were married with less than $1,000 to our name.

## The Reality Check

That's when we transitioned into the life of the masses. I was working a $7.00/hour construction job, and Nicole worked a $4.25/hour job at the front desk of a local fitness center. Everything moved so fast. We lived in the moment and forgot the promise that we could be anything when we grew up. We did what most twenty-somethings start to do when they discover life's hard—we settled.

I've learned that though everyone dies when they grow old, some choose to allow their dreams to die much earlier, typically in their twenties or early thirties. They give up their hopes and dreams, and despite the fact they still draw breath, they die internally. That pretty much describes my twenties. I quit exploring. I gave up the dream of baseball and entered the life I saw everyone else around me living–a life of settling. I began to drown in a nine-to-five life of quiet desperation and mere existence.

Like most, I thought the life I had settled for was normal. Only one percent get to live the life of their dreams. Right?

My father and grandfather worked in real estate and construction, so naturally, I entered the trade. For seven years, I made a living building houses. Nicole and I had three beautiful children during those years, and we had a good life. Still, the waves kept coming.

WITHOUT VISION
THE PEOPLE PERISH.
PROVERBS 29:18

Without realizing it, I had abandoned my previous life's vision–Major League

Baseball–without picking up a new, compelling one. A lack of vision means we give up a life of thriving and succumb to simply existing. God didn't create us for a life like that. Each of us were designed to create, to contribute, to serve and impact others. We were created for an exciting life, a life of passion and purpose. God didn't just save us from the bad, he called us to be on a mission for the good.

When people settle, it's as if they are in a little boat in the middle of the ocean with no destination in mind. When the storm comes—and they certainly will—we have no bearing for which way is true north. The waves toss us and take us under. Only a clear vision will provide direction, and without one we have no idea which way is up.

That's where I found myself after a few years of working with my dad. I started realizing the construction business was not for me, and the rocky relationship I've had with my dad most of my life didn't improve. So, as the waves began to rise, I looked into becoming a California Highway Patrol (CHP) Officer in order to escape the relational dynamics in our Central California home town.

The age cut-off for entering the CHP at the time was thirty-one, so the twenty-five-year-old me had a short window to complete the two-year application and testing process and hope to be among the one percent the force statistically would hire and send to their twenty-seven week, live-in, bootcamp style academy. I was excited to make it and had a lot of fun for five years. But even this new, exciting position didn't calm the waves.

## Cardboard Boats

When Nicole and I met, she was a healthy, vibrant, energetic, college athlete. But during those CHP years, my beautiful wife began to struggle to get out of bed. Caring for herself became a challenge, and chasing after our three young children grew nearly impossible. I felt completely helpless. Wasn't it my job to protect these precious people? Shiftwork prevented me from being there for her the way I wanted to be, so in a desperate attempt to help her, I encouraged Nicole to go to the doctor. They diagnosed her with chronic fatigue and fibromyalgia. At the time I thought nothing could be more painful than hearing those words, "There's really nothing we can do for you." His only advice was to find some "good" food supplements and a wish for "good luck."

Nicole continued to struggle with this debilitating condition. For two years, she visited countless doctors and tried even more supplements and shakes. People seemed to come out of the wood-work with suggestions. However, none offered any noticeable improvement. Instead of getting better, she got worse and developed additional health issues including significant hormonal imbalances. It was a very rough season for us. Out of des-peration she eventually resorted to prescription medications for depression, IBS and insomnia. Two of the medications she tried had unpleasant side effects. We didn't know what to do, and I felt like I was fighting the winds and the waves with a cardboard boat.

All over the United States, Cardboard Boat races offer spectators a chance to either laugh or be amazed. Participants build seacraft out of heavy-duty cardboard boxes. They paint them in a variety of themes, and in New Richmond, Ohio, home of the Cardboard Boat Museum and Inter-national Cardboard Boat Regatta, prizes include endurance, creativity, and of course, the Titanic award for the boat that offers fans the most dra-matic sinking episode. [6] Because let's face it, these things are crafted from refrigerator boxes—even

---

[6]    *Village of New Richmond* "The Art and Science of Cardboard Boats." accessed June 10, 2023. http://www.newrichmond.org/cardboard-boat-museum.html.

the most elaborately decorated, museum worthy boat will eventually sink.

*About one month after this photo was taken and three months before I met her, my wife, Nicole, who grew up in an atheistic home, gave her life to Christ and was baptized at this same beach where I nearly drowned.*
*(see Morro Rock above her head)*

Nicole, who had grown up in an atheistic home, had given her life to Christ just before I met her. In fact, I find it quite interesting that she was baptized in the same water near Morro Rock that nearly took my life months earlier.

I'd grown up in church, but my prayer for "salvation" had been that of a five-year-old given the choice between heaven or hell. "Of course, I'll take heaven," I said. They taught me all the rules, and I put on the mask of a Christian. Somehow my cardboard boat religion convinced Nicole and her newfound faith in Christ that mine was real.

## Just Add Duct Tape

Just before I got out of police work, I finally surrendered my life to Christ, but my return to construction didn't fix the holes in my makeshift boat. God had begun to transform my life; however, I continued to steer our cardboard ship toward the hope of a thirty-year retirement followed by a small, self absorbed vision of fishing my golden years away in the little-known tranquility of Northeastern California. In hindsight, I realize now what happened. I'd finally just come to the end of myself. Surrendering my hopes, my plans, my will, and my life to Jesus, and trusting him to give me the best plan for my life gave me a great start. However, I had a lot to learn (and still do).

Like adding Duct tape to a sinking cardboard boat, we kept looking for quick fixes. Earlier, we had believed moving away from extended family issues would be the best way to fix the holes. We tried to escape to Arkansas even before we had children, and when I started in the California Highway Patrol we relocated hours away. Still, something was missing. The emptiness that comes with a lack of vision haunted me.

My thought process went something like this: *This is not working. I'm not happy. I've got a great job, a beautiful wife, and three healthy kids. I even have the truck of my dreams - a 1993 F250 7.3L diesel pickup.* Some people might think it's not much, but these things were everything I wanted at the time. *Why do I still feel so empty?* My cardboard boat had begun to sink. I knew I couldn't go on living that way. I wanted to sail free and ride the waves with ease, but the boat I had at that time forced me to hug the shore and often bail water.

I honestly thought when I landed a good superintendent job with an Atlanta homebuilder we may have found the elusive Utopia I had been searching for. I was wrong.

Thankfully by this time, we'd discovered an answer to prayer—some little known yet highly effective whole-food supplements—and within six months, Nicole's body had completely healed itself. It never ceases to amaze me how incredible the human body is at self-correcting and performing as designed when given adequate nutrition. Unfortunately, our commercially grown food and highly processed diets lack many of these important nutrients.

As the storm of Nicole's health subsided, our nine-year-old daughter Savannah developed extended uncontrollable seizures. We spent an entire week in Atlanta Children's Hospital with her head hooked up to a jillion electrodes. Sometimes I think the unknown may be the scariest of waves. The doctors had no idea what brought them on. And even after giving her their best medicine, they could not find a way to get the continual seizures to stop. It was a very difficult time for our family.

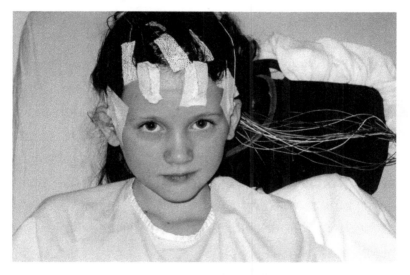

Our 9 year old daughter Savannah at the
Atlanta children's hospital being treated for seizures.

For three months, Savannah's seizures were so bad she couldn't even be homeschooled. I thought watching helplessly as my wife struggled was diffi-cult, but seeing one of your babies lying there with wires coming out of her head was in some ways worse. I just wanted to fix everything, but no one had a solution.

Thankfully, the same food supplements God led us to that had helped Nicole's body heal itself provided the answer to prayer for Savannah's seizures. It didn't happen overnight, and the journey to healing was extremely trying, but our little girl saw a full recovery over the months that followed and continues to be seizure-free to this day more than fifteen years later.

In the meantime, I had to provide for my family. I had made arrangements with the owner of the company I worked for to take on construction work on the side on my time off. We had come to an agreement on the kind of work I would take on, and I promised it would not interfere with the projects I was managing for him. I diligently made sure I was never double dipping or in competition with his company.

Everything was running smoothly. I had my first home construction about halfway done, and all of his projects were progressing as promised. And that's when the builder flipped out. At age 34, with six others to provide for, I was unemployed. Just like that. Even though I was wrongfully terminated, I had no recourse. Talk about a scary season for our lives. Our family had been rapidly expanding and we found ourselves with five children, very little in savings, and no steady income. Our situation would have qualified us for nearly every government assistance program available. Completely humbled, these waves were beating me up. I had no four year degree and no plan for the future. I felt like a failure.

I ended up starting my own construction company from scratch, and God worked it out, but the fear for my family during that season was real. Without a vision, I sank further into the crashing waves. I had moved the family to Atlanta to save them from the riptides that my dad created in California, but nothing stopped the relentless swells. My cardboard boat life had nothing to keep it seaworthy, and my foolish attempts at repairing the holes just increased the misery and left us more vulnerable.

# CHAPTER TWO
# THE BACKUP BOAT™

*Because of a lack of vision and life planning,
people arrive at the end of their life at a destination
determined solely by their circumstances
rather than by their intentionality.*

P erhaps that's where you are today. You feel
like you're in a cardboard boat with duct
tape protection and life's waves just keep
coming. Let me tell you a little secret we learned
the hard way: You can't outrun the waves. In fact,
not even the backup plan can save you. In order to
survive the storms we need something bigger.

Though we'd had three changes of location in
California during the highway patrol years as well
as the major move to the other side of the United
States, relocating hadn't been the answer. Every
new venue gave us a temporary sense of freedom,

but no one ever told us the idyllic life we searched for didn't exist, or if they did, we didn't believe them. We still believed those highlight reels. Certain we could outrun the storms and avoid the floods, we soon realized our backup plan meant we were merely treading water.

## Drifting at Sea

Those who succeed in professional sports or pursue music and acting careers usually don't have a backup plan. Though only a small percentage of those who head into those areas make it, the ones who do, have a strong vision, and they stick to it. They don't build an escape hatch into their dream. Instead they spend a lot of years preparing for and building a boat sturdy enough to withstand the elements.

Unfortunately, I didn't have any real plan in place, and I had never considered the option of a God-given vision to help me through. I let the winds and the waves carry me in whatever seemed like the next logical direction. Working with my dad seemed practical, but the decision didn't come with any long-term planning or heartfelt desire. Even the route for a planned thirty-year California Highway Patrol career lacked a significant vision.

To those who didn't know any better, everything looked picture perfect. But the breakers grew bigger and more torrential, and all I could do was watch the waves crash around us. It didn't take long for the world to see that my backup boat was more like a life raft than a second yacht fit to fight the waves.

> OUR LIFE IS NOT AFFECTED AS MUCH BY WHAT HAPPENS TO US AS MUCH AS IT IS AFFECTED BY HOW WE REACT TO WHAT HAPPENS TO US.

Perhaps you feel the same. You had big plans, but life happened. Believe it or not, embracing the waves can be life altering. I know people who live in denial of their past. They won't admit they have places in their life that need adjustments, and they'll never apologize for the hurt they've caused. Worse still, they cling to the hurts and ways they've been wronged, blaming others and their past for their present and making it virtually impossible for them to see any kind of vision for their future.

Life is full of obstacles, and you will always face challenges. However, recognizing and identifying the waves helps us move forward. Taking ownership of our past allows us to seize the swell and live in freedom.

Sadly, too many people settle for a life of aimless drifting. Without a vision for the future, they bob in the waves and allow even the smallest things to influence them, tugging them around even if it's pulling them in the wrong direction.

That's where Nicole and I were when we made the decision to leave Atlanta. You'd have thought all the waves we experienced would have pushed us to build our ark, but the rains kept coming, and we continued to drift in our little lifeboat.

When the housing market crashed in 2008, it hit my dad's construction company hard, and he was not able or willing to continue the business amidst the storm. He told me that if I didn't come back to run the company, he would either try to sell it or just shut it down. So, I allowed the tugboat to push me back to California in late 2008. My dad and my phenomenal uncle Warren made me CEO of the then struggling company. As we worked to turn the company around and make it profitable again, I slowly became part owner along with my younger brother Kevin and two younger cousins, Brent and Eric.

Meanwhile, in an effort to protect my immediate family from the challenges that still existed with my extended family in central California, I moved Nicole and our six children to Washington State near the Canadian border. I thought we'd be better off in that remote area. However, this meant I spent four days a week in California away from my family managing the construction company and additional time spent flying between the two locations.

Despite the fact that much larger national builders were filing bankruptcy during that difficult post-2008 housing market, we thrived with a quick pivot into a company that bought, renovated and sold houses. For many years we "flipped" about twenty homes each month. While I thought my career was helping my family, in reality, it was dragging us under. The money was good, but I missed many dinners, birthdays and sporting events, and though we'd found a remedy for Nicole's illnesses and our daughter's seizures had subsided, the next waves were about to hit.

## The Hardest Hitting Wave

If money could buy joy, we should have been ecstatic. The flipping business exploded, but everything important was falling apart.

While in Washington State, our fourteen-year-old daughter Dakota purchased a rescue horse. I happened to be home that weekend when she foolishly accepted a dare from her older sister Lacey and decided to ride the horse bareback after dark. We rushed her to the ER after it bucked her off

> EVEN A NEGATIVE SITUATION HOLDS THE POTENTIAL TO PRODUCE A POSITIVE PURPOSE.

and kicked her in the face. The impact broke her jaw and her sinus cavity, but that wasn't the worst news.

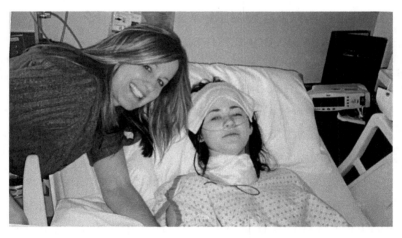

*My wife, Nicole, with our 14-year-old daughter Dakota in the hospital following thyroid cancer surgery.*

As if Nicole's health challenges and Savannah's seizures weren't bad enough, we now faced the hardest hitting wave of our life. While they were doing the scan to assess the damage, they saw a lump on Dakota's thyroid. The medical staff recommended we have it checked after her current injuries healed.

We learned that our precious teenage daughter had an aggressive form of papillary thyroid cancer that had already spread to twenty-two of her lymph nodes. Never in my wildest dreams did I think I'd ever hear those words spoken about one of my children. I kept wondering why her, why us? We couldn't understand how this could happen to our family. Hadn't we already faced enough?

This was a very aggressive kind of cancer, and the scariest time of our life. I'm not sure how we would have faced it without our faith. For months we were powerless. We could do nothing but pray and trust God to bring her through it. But it taught us a very valuable lesson.

The night we visited the ER because of her riding accident, we were devastated. Her healing took a great deal of time. But the truth is if the horse hadn't kicked her, she'd never have had that scan. That cancer would have continued to grow. Because it was such an aggressive cancer, by the time it would have been found by other means, we might not have Dakota with us today, cancer-free, married, and thriving 13 years later.

We didn't realize it at the time, and even while our daughter was going through the cancer treatments, praise was difficult. However, that unimaginable experience taught us to appreciate the big waves. We learned to praise God for that horse and even the crushed sinus cavity because it allowed doctors to find a tumor that might have taken her from us prematurely.

Dakota's cancer helped me realize that we all see only a partial picture of our lives and futures while God sees the bigger picture perfectly. Though these months were some of the hardest I've endured, I learned the importance of trusting Him and His promises no matter what the situation may look like at the moment. I rest in His promise that He'll never leave us or forsake us and that He'll never allow us to face anything we can't handle with Him. (1 Corinthians 10:13)

## Bigger Than Your Bank Account

Most define success by the number on your paycheck and other materialistic things—large bank accounts, investments, fancy cars, nice clothes, luxurious vacations, and impressive houses. Others try to demonstrate success with extreme overspending, high debt, and a relentless stress load. I learned the hard way that success can by no means be limited to numbers in a ledger. In fact, I've decided that monetary success accompanied by failure in other more important areas of life is not a successful life at all.

> MONEY IS CERTAINLY NECESSARY, AND ONE MEASURE OF SUCCESS, BUT OUR PURPOSE MUST BE DEEPER THAN JUST MONEY IN ORDER TO FIND FULFILLMENT AND JOY IN OUR WORK.

The world would have described my life as amazingly successful. Meanwhile, I was miserable. I had entered the darkest period of my life. I was missing life with my family and my spiritual life was failing. Nothing was going the way I hoped. I began to question everything I was doing and began drinking to escape. So, when my father walked out on my mother, I couldn't handle it.

Even though my dad and I have had a rough relationship since my teen years, I often call my childhood home a *Leave it to Beaver* existence. Dad and Mom took us to church every Sunday. I memorized scripture and felt extremely loved. I couldn't have asked for a better childhood. My parents claimed to be Christians and taught us that marriage was 'till death do us part.' Their relationship was like a rock to our family. No matter what happened, we knew we could count on Dad and Mom to be there.

My parents had been married for more than four decades, my dad owned the construction company, and his name was well-known in the small town where I grew up. Additionally, my grandfather owned a real estate agency. His brokerage had For Sale signs on so many pieces of property that when I was a kid, my friends thought the Blains owned the entire city, although that certainly was not the case. Despite my father's apparent success, none of it was enough.

Never in my wildest dreams could I have imagined how deeply their divorce would affect me and my siblings. I was the oldest, and we ranged in age from forty-three to thirty-seven. It rocked our world. When I found out my father was cheating on my mother and leaving her, I was crushed emotionally and mentally.

The ordeal sent my mom into a debilitating multi-year depression. I had to help her navigate the legal mess, and then I had to watch her sink deeper and deeper until she was bedridden and unable to function. For nearly a decade she endured what she now calls her great depression.

My dad's poor choices and all that he did to my mom created a dismal and distressing season for our entire family. And while my parent's divorce was only one of many factors, it played a part in the loss of my beautiful and vivacious thirty-nine--year-old younger sister, Amber.

She had it all–a loving husband, happy family, great church family, and more—no one would have expected her to be so distraught she would take her life. Yet, that's what she did. Everyone was shocked. She obviously suffered from mental illness; however, her friends and family, myself included, all would have put her in the 'not that bad' category.

My entire extended family was doing well financially; however, the money wasn't enough. It didn't keep my dad from leaving and it didn't comfort my mom after he left. My sister's bank account, loving husband, and exceptional four children couldn't save her from the waves that she faced, and my own successful business endeavors couldn't rescue me from the storms I was creating for myself.

The loss of my sister was the piece of straw that toppled the load. Life's storms were pulling me under fast. Like pain pills–they don't get rid of the pain, they merely mask it–my numbing agents only added to the problem. Waves of guilt and grief kept knocking me down. Nicole didn't even know how bad it had gotten, but she would soon find out, and the wave that threatened to end me became the one that God used to bring me topside again.

## Limited Success Leads to Limited Joy

Mark 8:36 says, "What good is it for someone to gain the whole world, yet forfeit their soul?" Most people believe success is found in a bigger bank account, a more prestigious title, and some form of notoriety. But I believe success includes great mental and physical health, strong, thriving relationships, and a personal relationship with Jesus Christ,

It took me some time to learn this lesson, but I found that when we keep our priorities aligned with God's wonderful plans there's no reason we cannot go after success in all these important areas and live a truly God-honoring, relationally rich, financially free, successful life.

When we settle for monetary bounty at the exclusion of more important things, we lose what's most critical in life. Jesus promised us abundance. We were created for more than mediocrity. All the things we all desire—unlimited love, joy, peace, goodness, and more wait for everyone who chooses to embrace true success rather than continue to simply tread water in the striving for more money and things.

Even though I was definitely growing in my faith, I still followed the wind and the waves instead of rowing toward the safety of Christ's shore. I discovered that the distractions of money, helping my extended family, and struggling to survive created a life of treading water.

Treading water is exhausting. You constantly move all your limbs but go nowhere. The goal is to merely keep afloat. Treading water while you fight the tides will leave you tired. However, treading water when the waves hit can be deadly.

> FAILURE IS A BRUISE
> NOT A TATTOO
> - JON SINCLAIR

Professionally I was killing it. The tax returns looked amazing. But after facing all those waves, dealing with our firstborn, Lacey, as she struggled with addiction, and watching my mother continue to suffer, I was done. I felt like a failure as a husband and father. My career seemed meaningless, and the internal pain had become more than I could bear. I remember telling Nicole, "I love you. I don't want to leave YOU, but I don't want to be here anymore. I just want to go to a faraway place, sit on a beach, and drink my life away." I realize that sounds silly, immature, unloving, and even illogical, but that was how much pain I was in. I'm not proud of it, but that was my reality then. The aimlessness of treading water had become more than I could take. Something had to give, and I knew if I didn't find a better boat, that something would be me.

# PART TWO

# RISING ABOVE
# THE WAVES

*To realize our full potential,*
*each of us must be willing to embrace our own unique*
*God -given attributes and be all that we can be.*

# CHAPTER THREE
# THRIVING IN THE WAVES

*Regardless of the obstacle,*
*we must intentionally choose to be a proactive overcomer*
*rather than a helpless victim of our circumstance.*

That dark period turned out to be the turning point in my life. Sharing my heart with Nicole opened the door to healing. Holding on to those feelings and putting on a brave face allowed the poison of the pain to eat at my soul like a flesh eating parasite. Restoration wasn't immediate–waves I couldn't see yet were on the horizon; however, recognizing and admitting my problem to another human became an outlet for the infection.

At Morro Rock, the waves had knocked me around, and when I couldn't fight them anymore, I gave up. That's sort of where I found myself as I poured my heart out to my wife. Mentally and spiritually I had sunk as low as I could go, and giving up allowed my feet to touch the bottom. I began to evaluate my life and really consider what God wanted for it rather than what the next logical move should be. And that allowed me to push off the bottom.

Unfortunately, I had created some ground-swells of my own that had repercussions I had yet to face.

## Fighting For the Surface

I share my story hoping someone who hears it won't end up nearly drowning like I did—either time. At Morro beach, I should have kept my buddy closer, paid attention to those more experienced than myself, and securely fastened my gear. During those commuting years, I could have followed a very similar strategy. I should have reached out to my friends when I felt myself going under instead of trying to escape in alcohol. If I'd bothered to ask for advice, I'm sure a pastor, counselor, or someone who'd walked life's journey longer would have given me some warning about the danger of missing out on family life, spreading myself too thin, and lacking a passion-filled purpose driven career.

I started the trek to the hard waves like most people—a drink now and then to destress. Eventually, the alcohol numbed the pain. I never worried about it becoming too much, because I was certain I had it under control.

When I was taken to jail for driving while intoxicated, it was Morro Rock all over again. I was sinking fast, and the water just kept getting darker and darker. The night of my arrest, I was supposed to fly home. We were always so excited to see each other since I worked out of town several days each week. Nicole stayed awake worrying because I hadn't called her like always before boarding the plane back home each week. The next day, her relief that I wasn't dead didn't keep her from being distraught about me spending the night in jail.

Emotions flooded my soul. A self-professed Christian, I knew I had let down so many people. On top of that, I had previously been that patrol officer that had arrested drivers for drinking and driving. I knew the dangers better than most. Embarrassed, foolish, humbled . . . I can't begin to list the torment that plagued me.

Because my blood alcohol level was nearly three times the

> SETBACKS ARE A SET UP FOR A GREATER IMPACT WITH YOUR COMEBACK.

legal limit, the judge sentenced me to a thirty-day inpatient rehab. The day I checked in, I experienced one of the most humbling moments of my life. Just before handing over my phone, I sent a text to sixty-five of my closest family, friends and associates letting them know why they wouldn't be able to reach me for the next thirty days. As I sat in that parking lot at the rehab facility humiliated to the core, guilt washed over me as I realized Nicole would have to run our new business and care for six kids on her own. Although I had given up all alcohol months before entering the rehab, I knew that if I wanted my life to be different, I had to change. I could not keep ignoring the waves hoping they would go away.

The repercussions of that DUI still haunt me. A few years ago, I took hours and hours of flight training. I really wanted to pilot a small engine plane. Just before my solo, flying alone without anyone else aboard, my instructor sent me to get the required physical exam. The doctor's words were like a boulder crushing my dream.

"Allan, you are the epitome of health. In fact, you are the healthiest person I've not been able to pass for a flight physical."

The previous DUI I disclosed on the medical questionnaire, with a blood alcohol level that high automatically disqualified him from passing me to pilot a plane alone. It didn't matter how many years ago it was. Crashing waves leave devastation, especially when beach people ignore the warnings. I could have spent a lot of time and money proving to the Federal Aviation Administration (FAA) that I don't have a problem with alcohol anymore, and though I had abstained from all alcohol for a substantial length of time, I decided not to pursue it. Maybe someday, but for now, the experience reminds me of the folly of ignoring the waves.

## The Wave Is Not the Enemy

Several years earlier, struggling with the dread of complacency and recognizing the fact that I was going through the motions at church had convinced me I should start reading the book I had based my faith on. Slow and incremental changes marked the next ten years. It started with me making a full commitment to Jesus. I recognized that the prayer I offered at five had simply been a request for "fire insurance." I was missing the best part of the Christian life – giving my life to the one who was able to empower me with the ability to live a truly successful life of freedom!

Reading scripture also confirmed that waves are inevitable. John 16:33 revealed the truth. "I have told you these things so that in Me you may have peace. You will have suffering in this world. Be courageous! I have conquered the world." Coming to terms with the fact the perfect life I had been looking for wasn't available this side of heaven wasn't easy. However, learning to see the three phases of life's waves made a huge difference.

A wave watcher understands the swells and troughs of the sea. Wave mapping allows scientists to forecast the size of the waves at any given beach—a gift for surfers. Even the novice surfer knows the three phases of the wave. You are either heading into the wave, in the middle of the wave, or exiting the wave. And if you don't recognize the three phases, the waves will likely toss you around, pull you under, and drain the fun out of the experience.

Life offers those same phases. When we begin to understand how the waves work and what the different phases look like, we can conquer the waves, rise high on the swells, and come out safely on the other side. Just like on a beach, some waves last longer and provide more opportunities for a wipeout. However, with practice and by surrounding ourselves with people who have experience with the storms, we can catch the wave and ride smoothly.

Riptides are a bit different. Only experienced beachcombers can spot them. They hide between the waves, and the water looks calm. But if you get caught in one, you find it's anything but tranquil. Nicole's illnesses, Savannah's seizures, Dakota's cancer, and my dad and mom's divorce were like riptides in my life. They caught me off guard, and because I had little experience with navigating life's waves, they nearly pulled me under.

As we navigated all those storms, I began to see that while I can't avoid the waves, I can prepare for them. In fact, I discovered that waves have the potential to propel me to something bigger. Each time we enter a wave, we can learn how to ride the next one a bit better. After years of looking for peaceful waters, I eventually learned the truth–in Christ we can have peace and joy even in the middle of the storm.

> OUT OF ADVERSITY COMES OPPORTUNITY.
> ~ BENJAMIN FRANKLIN

Benjamin Franklin said, "Out of adversity comes opportunity." When I began to look at the waves as opportunities and potential, my ability to see the incoming waves heightened. And every time I walked through adversity, I exercised those muscles making them stronger for the next round.

I've faced a lot since that day at Morro Rock, and by the grace of God I've survived. Life has shown me that the waves we face spiritually, mentally, and relationally are scarier than the one that took me down in the Pacific Ocean. Recognizing my weaknesses and looking to God allowed Nicole and I to find the vision God had for us. The waves haven't subsided, but they don't frighten us anymore.

When we started our current life transformation business, I finally felt as though I had a vision that could carry my family safely through the storms. Life became purposeful and passion filled. I was doing something I felt truly mattered on a grand scale. All the best success strategies, tactics, positive mindsets, and money don't matter if a person loses their health. I saw plenty of evidence that most were not enjoying optimal health and vitality, and I knew we had to share our proven solution.

We had found a way to make an impact on those around us, give our family the freedom we craved, as well as scale and grow a business together with my best friend and love of my life, Nicole. This vision promised financial freedom as well as time and geographical freedom. As a family, our opportunities seemed unlimited. We had a cause much bigger than ourselves–helping others–, and I began to see the water grow lighter blue as I climbed closer to the Sun.

Within the first sixteen months of building this secondary income stream, we created a passive income that could support our family of eight. We loved what we were doing. We had witnessed these whole-food nutritional supplements help turn Nicole's health around fifteen years earlier, when nothing we'd previously tried had provided any measurable difference. Plus, they assisted our nine-year-old daughter Savannah through her spell of seizures, and successfully supported our daughter Dakota through her bout with cancer.

Now we use our home-based life transformation business to distribute the same products to help others improve their health. Additionally, we feel blessed to be able to assist people as they create their own online passive incomes and join our transformational, growth-minded, Christ-centered and supportive organization.

## Stop Trying to Escape and Ignore the Waves

Nearly two years later, Nicole and I hosted a three day training retreat for about one hundred members of our North American team. People traveled from all over the U.S. and Canada to attend. At 11:30 a.m., just a few hours before the event was scheduled to begin, the call came. My younger brother had taken his life. He had been one of the top Keller-Williams real estate agents in the nation and as far as any of us knew, happily married. I felt like I had just been punched in the gut. I struggled to maintain my composure.

The last thing I felt like doing was to forge ahead hosting this three day event. I wanted to find a hole and crawl in. People expected me to be on stage teaching, training, and motivating our team. Every person there had made a substantial investment of time and money. I was torn between honoring their investment and letting the wave carry me far away.

I called my family in California to check on them and went to prayer. Nicole and I decided we needed to honor our commitment in Washington State where we were hosting the event, and then we could get to California to support and mourn with the family after the event was over. During the opening session, since the news was already getting out, we let the team know what had happened. We told them we'd like to keep the focus on them and our purpose for the weekend and not talk about it, so that we could focus on serving them for the weekend.

One attendee, an extended family member, believed we'd made a bad decision. She thought we were awful for not leaving immediately to go to California. So in addition to the pain of losing my brother, we had to deal with the hurt of her toxic attitude and backstabbing comments to many others during the weekend. This was unbelievably difficult amidst the agonizing pain and tremendous stress I was under, but I am thankful God helped me to forgive her.

Getting through the three days was excruciating. I had been so blind-sided by the news. At the same time, I felt good about standing strong through this wave and carrying out the plan God had given me for the weekend. My life had purpose, and I knew that I could both live this calling the Lord had put on my life and honor my family too.

On a side note, I want to give a shout out for this beautiful transformational community God gave us. These phenomenal business partners honored our request to get through the weekend without talking about it, and then, though we were the hosts and leaders of this event, they offered us amazing comfort. I'm grateful God knows best where we should be, what we need, and when we need it. We just have to ask for His wisdom.

Carrying out God's vision isn't always easy. Often we have to choose between the logical or heart rending and God's call. I'm so thankful for God's promise in James 1:5 - "Now if any of you lacks wisdom, he should ask God-who gives to all generously and ungrudgingly-and it will be given to him." Going to be with my family three days earlier would have been a good plan, but staying at that event to share my story and encourage those in attendance, something that feels more like a ministry to us than a business, was God's plan. God's plan is always the best plan.

During our first thirty-one years of marriage, we moved twenty-two times. The first dozen or so fell into the category of trying to escape the waves, and while many of the others had more purpose, none had as much meaning as our last move, the one we made to follow our vision.

We had packed the U-Haul™ before we went to the retreat. The trailer, car, and RV all sat in the driveway of our eight acre Washington state home waiting to pull out and move to Nashville on Monday morning following that three day event. Instead, we all boarded a plane and attended my brother's funeral with my dwindling extended family. With Dad and Mom divorced, Mom not able to attend the funeral due to her severe bedridden depression, my two younger siblings gone, and the other sister in the middle of a felony trial that would send her to prison, the anguish and heartache I felt for my family might have been overwhelming if I hadn't developed a relationship with the One who keeps me safe in the storms and created a life vision for where I was going.

> EVERY ADVERSITY, EVERY FAILURE, EVERY HEARTACHE CARRIES WITH IT THE SEED OF AN EQUAL OR GREATER BENEFIT.
> - NAPOLEON HILL

The next week, we made the cross country move from Washington State to the Nashville, Tennessee area. The only person we knew in Tennessee was the realtor who sold us our home; however, we knew we'd finally chosen a location based on our passion and purpose and the bigger vision for our life. God had led us there the year before when Nicole and I packed the family into our forty-foot RV and made an 8,000 mile road trip across twenty-nine states, working our business while we searched and prayed for God to show us where he wanted us to land our boat.

I'll never forget, as different waves of life pounded and various life trials hit us, one of our mentors, Lawrence, often told Nicole and me, "Don't hit your heads on the ceiling, jumping for joy." He was referring to James 1:2 "Consider it a great joy, my brothers and sisters, whenever you experience various trials," in an effort to help remind us to keep a proper perspective. Some of the men and women I have met who have the deepest wells of knowledge, wisdom, and character have been through some of the most difficult and trying situations in life. It is in the midst of the storm that we learn, grow, develop our capabilities, and increase confidence as we eventually reach the other side of the storm. You see, it's not success that strengthens our character, but rather the adversity we face and the way we react to it. Each instance molds us into the person we desire to be—a person equipped to lead and help others on a whole new level.

Today, more than five years after our move to Tennessee, we have more connections than we have time to cultivate, hundreds of acquaintances and so many wonderful close friends. We've been blessed beyond measure. However, we'd have missed those blessings if we hadn't been willing to surrender our original small vision and pick up the much bigger, more adventurous one God had for us. Ours made sense. It was driven by logic and a feeble attempt to stay in control of providing for our family. God's, though less traditional, gives us more security, more freedom, more adventure, and more peace.

Even with all of that, the waves still come, and we feel blessed that we can help you understand better how to ride them.

## Thriving Through the Waves

Reading scripture showed me truth, and Nicole's faith, patience, forgiveness and prayers allowed me to develop a different perspective on life.

Thriving through the waves means looking at them from a new vantage point. We now see them as opportunities rather than the enemy. Plus, we understand the waves are going to just keep coming. You can try to escape them. You can even pretend to ignore them. But if you do, you're just going to get knocked down.

I think of three amazing celebrities who've learned how to

> IT'S A CHOICE EVERY DAY TO EITHER GROW AND IMPROVE OR TO STAGNATE AND DECLINE.

ride the waves. Nick Vujicic was born without arms and legs. He had every right to try to stay away from the excitement of the ocean and wallow in self-pity. Instead, he sees what others call limitations as opportunities. He brings hope to hundreds of thousands each year as he takes the stage and shares his story as well as the story of what Jesus Christ has done in his life.

Joni Eareckson-Tada didn't get hit by a breaker; she dove into the Chesapeake Bay after misjudging the depth of the water. More than fifty years ago, the diving accident left her paralyzed from the neck down. Rather than let the waves keep knocking her over, she chose to use her limitations to propel her to fame—though I don't think becoming famous was her goal at the time. She chooses to be a living example of how God can redeem broken things. Author, artist, and speaker, her pain has been an inspiration and encouragement to countless individuals. Today, her non-profit, Joni & Friends, provides wheelchairs, Bibles, retreats, and getaways to special needs persons and their families.

Finally, a true wave rider continues to surf even after she lost an arm in a shark attack. Not many would know Bethany Hamilton's name if she had given up staying on top of the waves after her traumatizing experience at age thirteen. Now a mom with kids of her own, I'm inspired to see her help others become Unstoppable despite life's trials.

## You Can Thrive Through the Waves

I've learned to thrive despite the waves. It's still not easy, but it's better than letting them knock you down time after time. Nicole and I have made it our mission to help others navigate the storms and ride the swells that try to drag them under.

As you begin to learn the Life's Hard Succeed Anyway philosophy, I want to offer you some definitive steps you can take to thrive despite life's waves. Having the courage to commit to action will catapult you to your first taste of success.

- **Fight for the Surface.** Hopefully, you won't allow yourself to get pulled under as far as I did. If you're using any kind of addiction or distraction of any kind as an escape, get help today. Don't wait until you're so weak that you hit bottom.
- **Remember the Wave is Not the Enemy.** Follow God's call even when it's hard. It won't always make sense to those around you, but in the end, you'll be blessed.

- **Stop Trying to Escape and Ignore the Waves** and lose the excuses. Making excuses rarely if ever results in success. When we own our mistakes and focus on results rather than running from the hard things in life, we can make progress.
- **Thrive Through the Waves.** It's time to reset your perspective. I jump started my reset with scripture. The foundation of success is in your beliefs. Your belief will set the stage for your success.
  - o Don't let self-doubt or fear paralyze you. *Do not be anxious about anything, but in every situation, by prayer and petition, with thanksgiving, present your requests to God. - Philippians 4:6*
  - o Begin to monitor your thoughts. *We demolish arguments and every pretension that sets itself up against the knowledge of God, and we take captive every thought to make it obedient to Christ. - 2 Corinthians 10:5*
    *[2] Do not conform to the pattern of this world, but be transformed by the renewing of your mind. Then you will be able to test and approve what God's will is—his good, pleasing and perfect will. - Romans 12:2*

o Do you focus on negative or positive? By focusing on the positive, you can rise above the waves and succeed.

*Finally, brothers and sisters, whatever is true, whatever is noble, whatever is right, whatever is pure, whatever is lovely, whatever is admirable—if anything is excellent or praiseworthy—think about such things. - Philippians 4:8*

# CHAPTER FOUR
# THE STAGING AREA

I want to help you build a boat sturdy enough to withstand the waves, but before we can create anything of substantial size, we must make space. Noah probably had to find a large level spot and clear trees to make room for the large structure God had described. Likewise, many things had to happen in my life before I could stay afloat and live out the vision the Creator had prepared for me.

First and foremost, I had to change my understanding of success. As I mentioned previously, the world's definition of success will never bring true satisfaction. Those who strive for money, status, and notoriety miss the best things in life. The truly successful have found contentment in every area of their lives. Regardless of the size of their investments, they feel like they have enough. They never go out of their way to alienate people; however, this rare breed doesn't let their relationships determine their happiness. They never have to go to work; they want to go to work. Their diet and exercise regimen aren't forced on them, they enjoy being good stewards of their health. What some call limitations, the successful view as potential to be creative.

Contentment mustn't be confused with complacency. Contentment finds joy in the moment. Complacency settles for what life throws their way. Contentment strives for more but doesn't need more. Complacency gets lazy because it sees no hope in the future.

True success needs a vision to fulfill. But before we can really live out a God-sized vision, we need to cut down a few trees and make room for the boat.

## Unveiling Our True Identity

When a fighter gets hit hard, he often feels very disoriented and can't see well. At that moment, if he wants to stay in the fight, he has to fall back on his training. Likewise, when the waves of life hit, we need a solid foundation–the foundation of our identity.

I had to come to understand I was more than my father's son, or Nicole's husband. My identity couldn't be tied up in the way I earned money or even my work ethic. I began to believe Zig Ziglar's statement, "You are designed for achievement, engineered for success, and endowed with seeds of greatness."

Think of yourself as a Rembrandt or a Picasso, a symphonic concerto or a cello solo. Paintings and musical compositions don't do anything in and of themselves. Their value is inherently tied to their creators.

The same is true of you. Your greatness is dependent on the One who made you, and His Word makes it clear that you are precious and have potential that goes beyond what any human can imagine. Jeremiah 1:5 tells us we were chosen, set apart, and appointed even before we were born. Psalm 139:14 says we were fearfully and wonderfully made.

As I began to realize that my heavenly Father thought I was phenomenal even with all my failures, my confidence increased, and I was better able to handle the waves.

Laying the foundation of understanding our identity paves the way for us to build an ark that will ride the waves. But the secret to believing your worth in Christ is in changing your mindset.

## Changing Your Mindset

Nearly every battle is won or lost in the six inches between our ears. Waves hit everyone. No one gets to choose which waves come, when they hit, or how high they swell. You do get to choose your reaction to them, and your identity, the way you view yourself, plays a big part in the way you handle the wave. It has been said that there are those who think they can and those who think they can't, and both are correct.

One of the big things that steals our chance at thriving is the victim mindset. I see far too many fall into this trap. Before we can start to build our ark, we have to give up blaming circumstances and other people for the waves. Nicole and I could have easily gotten caught up in the 'poor me' mentality as she and the girls struggled. When my parents divorced and my siblings took their lives, we had every right to feel victimized. It's not as if we never asked, "Why me?" I already shared with you that for a season I lived in that dark place of victim mentality. But when things got dark and the waves started taking me under, I eventually remembered my foundation. I am a victor because Jesus Christ is on my side.

The victim mentality steals dreams and robs our joy. The obstacle may be self-inflicted or come from external sources, either way, we must choose whether we will enter the wave a victim or a victor. The waves will come, but with the help of Christ, you can beat them— even the waves that threaten to knock you over.

> YOU CAN'T DEPOSIT EXCUSES.

Victors don't make excuses. Believe me, I know from firsthand experience, they won't serve you well. By focusing on solutions and results rather than looking for the reason for failure, we can make progress. We might need a change in schedule or a new self-discipline. Victors never "fail", they simply evaluate what didn't work so they can move ahead with a better plan. What do you need to adjust in your life to set yourself up for success?

Victors aren't afraid to ask for help. Admitting our plan doesn't work isn't declaring defeat. God has placed us in the midst of friends and family with a variety of talents and varying perspectives and insights, and often one of them will have the solution to our dilemma—a solution we will never find if we refuse to ask for help.

Moving into the victor mindset doesn't mean you won't encounter fear. Let's face it, a lot of those waves can be scary. But the victor mindset chooses to face the waves courageously. Courage is not the lack of fear. In fact, if you aren't afraid, you don't need courage. Courage sprouts from fear but only in the one who thinks like a victor.

Fear and faith share a common trait: both believe in a future that hasn't happened yet. The difference is that fear believes in a negative future, while faith believes in a positive one. Since neither has occurred, why wouldn't we choose to believe in a better future? What we believe makes a difference. If you believe your best days are behind you, they will be. But if you believe your best days are still to come, they are. Our beliefs have an impact, so it's important to choose to believe in the positive possibility and then work hard and make it happen.

I want you to give up the victim mindset so you aren't one of those people who abandon their dreams before they've given them a chance. Consider an elephant that's been chained to a stake from infancy. Since the elephant tried and couldn't break the chain when she was tiny, when it becomes an adult and possesses plenty of strength to do so, it won't even try. Much like those gentle giants, we allow ourselves to get caught up in the limitations of our past. Are you trapped in the idea that what you are doing now is all you can do because you can't see your capabilities? Or maybe you can't see that you've already outgrown your current situation.

Second Corinthians 10:5 tells us to take every thought captive. We can not allow those negative thoughts and past failures to control the way we think. If I had listened to my negative thoughts when I ran my first marathon (26.2 miles) at age 43, I'd have given in to the pain. My body screamed at me to start walking, but my mind told my body I could do it; I had trained well. I finished in three hours twenty-six minutes, averaging a seven-minute-fifty-two second mile pace over the course of those 26.2 miles on that ninety-three degree June day.

When we started our online side hustle from home, self-doubt threatened. My brain reverted to the familiar. I knew nearly everything about real estate and construction; however, staying in the safe shallow end would mean I'd have missed out on all the tremendous blessings I'm experiencing in the business we enjoy today.

We can overcome the waves by the way we talk to ourselves as we enter them. Entrepreneur and motivational speaker Jim Rohn shared some great wisdom when he put it this way.

> *"It's not what happens that determines your life's future, it's what you do about what happens....all of us are like little sailboats. It's not the blowing of the wind that determines our destination, it's the set of the sail.*
>
> *The same wind blows on us all. The wind of disaster, the wind of opportunity, the wind of change, the wind when it is favorable, the wind when it is unfavorable. The same wind blows on us all. The economic wind, the social wind, the political wind.*
>
> *The difference in where you arrive, the difference in where I arrive in one year, three years, or five years, is not the blowing of the wind but it's the set of the sail."*

Which direction will you set your sail?

When the voice and the vision on the inside is more profound, more clear, and louder than all the noise and opinions on the outside, you are well on your way to success.

# A Changed Mindset Means Acting With Confidence

Understanding your true identity and transforming the way you think naturally lead to acting on your new mindset. You'll begin to do and be more than you ever imagined. And with every action, you will find yourself with added confidence. You will more naturally have the courage to step out of your comfort zone, which permanently expands your comfort zone over time, and you'll find yourself choosing your companions with more care.

There is one dangerous riptide associated with confidence, and that's the temptation to let arrogance wear the mask of confidence. Arrogance is the fuel of the insecure. It needs to show off and boast. Confidence knows its strength but doesn't need anyone to see it.

Consider the fictitious character, Clark Kent. If he was arrogant, his whole crew would know he was Superman. Confidence allowed him to achieve all his goals, live the life of his dreams, and keep his super powers under wrap.

Confidence builds on a high intrinsic value. When you truly understand your identity and embrace who you are, especially who you are in Christ, you no longer stake your worth on your achievements, abilities, or accolades. Even in the midst of failure, fear, and feeling forsaken, the confident rise high above the waves. When your self worth is based on who you are rather than what you do or what others think of you, no one and nothing can take that from you.

Arrogance is steeped in comparison and feeling superior. Confidence only wants to outperform its last personal best. Arrogance is self-reliant, but confidence that is based in security in Christ understands that it can "do all things through Christ who strengthens me." (Philippians 4:13)

And perhaps the most tell-tale sign of arrogance versus confidence is the way they express success. Arrogance is boastful while confidence is expressed in gratitude.

## Developing an Attitude of Gratitude

Ark builders (Arkitects™) naturally become grateful for every experience. Studies show that being thankful makes people happier, improves relationships, and can potentially counteract depression and suicidal thoughts. Expressing gratitude can actually change your brain and boost self-esteem. Believe it or not, researchers have seen improved physical health in the more appreciative of the population. The oxytocin gratitude releases decreases inflammation, lowers blood pressure, and protects your heart. [7]

I start each day with a regimen of gratitude. Even before my feet hit the floor, I spend a minute or two intentionally thinking about many of the things I have to be thankful for. Any positive thing—regardless of its size—gets a spot in my thoughts. If I think about my marriage, it triggers a word of thankfulness. When the air conditioner kicks on, I remember how privileged I am to live in a world with such luxury. I praise God for my bed, the breath in my lungs, the incredible woman laying next to me, and the ability to sleep all night.

Then as I move throughout my day, I try very hard to continue the practice. Yes, I'm bound to get derailed at some point. Humanity sneaks in at the worst possible moments, but I've discovered that the more I practice gratitude, the easier it becomes to get my brain back on the right track. God knew what he was doing when he advised us to "give thanks in everything; for this is God's will for you in Christ Jesus" in 1 Thessalonians 5:18

The more developed the attitude becomes, the more you'll see how vital it is when the storms start

---

[7]  *University of Utah.* "Practicing Gratitude for Better Health and Well-being." November 19, 2021. (https://healthcare.utah.edu/healthfeed/2021/11/practicing-gratitude-better-health-and-well-being.

to rise. When the waves hit hard, sometimes the only thing we can be thankful for is our identity. As we cling to the edge of the ship, afraid the next swell will take us under, the words, "Thank you that I know I'm a child of God" can be the break in the clouds that helps us through the monsoon. It also helps me to remember that every challenge has the potential to put us in a position to encourage, inspire, and minister to others. Adversity can lead to bigger platforms where we can pronounce God's goodness and share our gratitude.

You can also use the power of appreciation to fuel someone else's boat. Being intentional about showering others with positive words can be life changing not only for you, but more importantly for the other person.

One day my friend, business partner and cousin Dwight Johnson and his father, my uncle, Burnell Johnson stopped by. In the middle of the conversation, they began to share their appreciation for our mutual friend, John. I thought, *I wish John could hear this.*

So, after Dwight and Burnell left, I hopped on Facebook Messenger and sent John a message to relay the positive things I'd heard about him. I could tell it meant a lot to John to hear those words. Plus, I got the added benefit of feeling good about what I had done and feeling appreciated by John for having passed along the compliment.

One study demonstrated that managers who pass along compliments see a significant increase in performance. In fact one of the teams that had been shown proper appreciation performed fifty percent better than the team that heard no affirmations.[8] How are you doing affirming others?

Appreciation costs little but time. Even a short text or the words 'thank you for . . .' or 'I sure appreciate you for . . .' can change a person's outlook. I've heard of a phone call or a positive word at just the right moment keeping someone with suicidal thoughts from taking the action they were contemplating. I still have saved voicemails from years ago that made such a positive impact in my life.

[8]  Burton, Linda Roszak. *Wharton Alumni Club* "Discovering the Health and Wellness Benefits of Gratitude" Accessed July 6, 2023) https://www.whartonhealthcare.org/discovering_the_health.

*Our firstborn, Lacey. Beautiful inside and outside.*
*Picture taken a few years ago before the addictions had*
*tightened their grip on her, causing her to choose*
*a life on the street.*

Life doesn't have to be perfect to be grateful. We have to learn to be appreciative of the good even when the harsh waves are still breaking in. Even as I write this one of our five daughters, Lacey, is lost in a world of drugs, alcohol and hard living. At age twenty-nine she chooses to remain living on the streets of Los Angeles, sleeping in parks, on benches, in tents, doing who knows what in order to continue her drug life though we've offered her rehabilitation on numerous occasions over the years. Though my heart breaks for her, and it's a constant reminder of all of my past shortcomings as a husband and father, I choose to remain grateful for the work God's done and continues to do in me and my family, and for all the wonderful things he has blessed me with in so many other areas of my life. I'm thankful I can trust Lacey to Him and His loving care for her and we hope to encourage other parents of children in active addictions of any kind.

Humans tend to be good at seeing what's broken, but with a bit of retraining we can see just as much good. Nicole and I could easily get stuck in worrying about Lacey and thinking the worst, but we've faced the fact that she's an adult. At twenty-nine, her life is her own, and we can't try to control the outcome of her waves. So we've decided to focus on what we can control—our own mindset. We've apologized to her for our past shortcomings and released them to God. We choose to show her love and pray for her, while looking for the good and being appreciative. It's all we can do.

When we learn to focus on gratitude and share the positive rather than the negative, we become expert wave riders, and our ark turns into a refuge for everyone in our wake.

# Getting the Staging Area Ready for Your Ark

In the next chapter we're going to begin to build a boat that will withstand every storm—even the hurricanes, tidal waves, and monsoons. But before we can tackle the enormous task of building an ark, we have to make certain we have our staging area ready.

- **Unveil Your True Identity.** I can't stress enough the importance of understanding who you are. I encourage you to check out these scriptures and read and write them until you are convinced of how precious, important, and vital you are to the Creator of the universe.
  - Psalm 139:13-14 (NIV) - For you created my inmost being;
    you knit me together in my mother's womb.
    [14] I praise you because I am fearfully and wonderfully made;
    your works are wonderful,
    I know that full well.
  - Romans 8:28 (NIV) - [28] And we know that in all things God works for the good

of those who love him, who have been called according to his purpose.

- o 1 Corinthians 2:16 (NIV) - But we have the mind of Christ.
- o Psalm 62:5 (NIV) - Yes, my soul, find rest in God; my hope comes from him.
- o Philippians 4:13 and 19 (NIV) 13 I can do all this through him who gives me strength. [19]And my God will meet all your needs according to the riches of his glory in Christ Jesus.
- o Psalm 28:7a (NIV) - The LORD is my strength and my shield;
  my heart trusts in him, and he helps me.

- **Transform Your Mindset.** What's the first thing you think in the morning and, quite possibly more important, your last thought before going to sleep and giving it to your subconscious to dwell on for hours? What do you feed your mind? Anytime you face a difficult obstacle, stop, reflect, and make sure you own responsibility for the outcome, then determine the best course of action to improve the situation. Think about what you are giving up if you choose the victim mindset. Let's continue this journey agreeing to leave the blame and pity parties on the deserted island of victim mentality. Because we're about to hoist the sails, embrace life's difficult waves, and succeed anyway.

- **Perform with Confidence.** Embrace your unique abilities and your worth in Christ. Commit to taking action even if you're fearful of the results. Remember, stepping out in the face of failure is the action of the courageous. Be so persistent in action that you don't have time to compare yourself to someone else or dwell in the land of superiority.
- **Develop an Attitude of Gratitude.** Begin and end each day with gratitude. Begin with things that others seem to ignore. Grab a notebook and create a Gratitude Journal. Additionally, share a word of appreciation for someone every day. Call, send a text, or write a handwritten note to a friend or a coworker to let them know why you appreciate them.

Now that the staging area is set, it's time to craft that compelling vision and build a boat that will carry you further than you can ever imagine.

# CHAPTER FIVE
# CRAFT A COMPELLING VISION

*"Build your ark before it rains"*

P rior to the 1950s, the world believed that running a four-minute mile was impossible. But Roger Bannister had a vision. As I understand it, conventional wisdom at that time believed that the heart couldn't handle running that fast for that long. Fortunately, Roger didn't buy into it. On May 6, 1954, the twenty-five-year-old Bannister ran as hard as he could and achieved the impossible.

More remarkably, after the young runner broke the record, though no one in recorded history had ever done it before, ten people broke the four-minute-mile mark in the twelve months that followed.

Within just ten years, three hundred sixty people accomplished the goal. Bannister's vision opened the door for hundreds of runners to create their own vision and become more than previously thought humanly possible.

Unfortunately, many prefer to believe the lie that the grass is always greener somewhere else. But do you know where the grass is always greener— wherever you water it. It reminds me of the old Native American parable. They say that a fight goes on inside every human. It's a terrible fight between two wolves. One is evil—full of anger, envy, misery, greed, arrogance, and ego. The other is good—filled with love, joy, peace, hope, generosity, truth, and faith. And the wolf you feed is the wolf that wins.

# Becoming an Arkitect™

During the time of Noah, the world chose to feed the evil wolf. Humanity had embraced darkness to the point God knew their hearts were beyond changing. Only Noah fed the good wolf, and walked in faith. So, God laid out a plan for him. If the five-hundred-year-old Bible hero had attempted an undertaking like an ark without some sort of "blueprint," he'd never have finished in time. Though others had built boats before, no one had attempted something this big.

When you set Noah's ark next to other prehistoric vessels, you get a vivid picture of the difference between a human vision and a God-given vision. Archeologists have unearthed fully preserved boats they believed to be from the time of Noah, but the largest one they've discovered is about 142 feet long. So, the ark, coming in at 510 feet, dwarfs the competition. It poses the question, do you want a vision of human or Godly proportions?

Your vision is a three part, clear and vibrant picture that includes what, why, and who. What you want to do (your mission), why you want to do it (your purpose) and who you want to share the vision with (your community)? Your mission will guide all your actions, your purpose will fuel your passion, and your community will provide the support and collaboration you need to succeed.

> IF YOU DON'T KNOW WHERE YOU'RE GOING, ANY ROAD WILL GET YOU THERE.
> ~ LEWIS CARROLL

A vision will give you a destination. By putting a plan in place, you not only have a roadmap to help you navigate the waves, you also have a tool to build a wavemap that will predict obstacles and roadblocks. But the key to the grandest vision is to let God give you the blueprint.

My journey with Christ began during my final years with the CHP, but I didn't really embrace my vision until a couple years before we moved to Nashville. Prior to that, it was tempting to craft a small, comfortable, easily attainable plan, but that's not a God-sized vision. As you begin to consider where you want your life to end up, grab that confidence we developed in the staging area and think big.

I can tell you from personal experience, building an ark takes time and effort. Even finding the vision God had for us took some work. We obviously traipsed off the path a time or two; nevertheless, God has used every experience to create good in our lives. And every step in perseverance has been worth it.

It's important to remember that success is guaranteed to those who don't quit. We were married twenty three years before we opened the door to God's ultimate plan, but finding our vision was the first step in Nicole and me building an international business that now includes thousands of people in numerous countries on multiple continents. A business that has seen countless lives positively transformed physically, financially and spiritually and produces millions of dollars in revenue each year. If you're interested in learning more about how our whole-food nutritional supplements may also benefit you or someone you love and care about, or any other aspect of our life transformation business, please send an email to support@AllanBlain.com with "Life Transformation Info Request" in the subject line or scan this QR Code.

It's much like the lesson from the Chinese bamboo farmer. A Chinese bamboo tree takes serious commitment and consistency to grow. It requires five years of daily care. The seed must be watered and fertilized each day without fail and without any satisfaction. For approximately 1,825 days the spot of dirt gets watered. When the seed finally sprouts, the bamboo tree grows ninety feet in just five weeks.

It would be easy for the farmer to give up before the tree peeked its head out of the dirt; however, consider the wonderful reward the farmer would miss if he quit too soon. Likewise, your plan will need a commitment to consistency.

I also want to emphasize that a vision committed to God can't fail. Proverbs 16:33 says, "Commit your activities (works) to the LORD, and your plans will be established." (CSB) That's an amazing promise. But receiving such an amazing promise will take a little work. Fortunately, you can learn from my mistakes as well as my successes. So, let's get busy and build this boat.

## It Begins With the Hull

Not every boat has a deck or a roof, but each one has a hull. Even canoes, kayaks, and catamarans require a watertight base to keep them afloat. If this foundational element lacks integrity, nothing else matters.

That's the reason every compelling vision has a huge why. Some would even consider it a calling. God called Noah to build a big boat. He called me to start a business that would be the catalyst to create an impact that would outlive me. The Vision Maker helped me craft a plan that calls me to live a life full of intention and meaning. I wake up every morning excited to see beyond the waves to find freedom and purpose so I can leave an impact by helping others better navigate the storms.

Discovering my calling began when my friend Josh Clark saw me treading water while we still lived in Washington State. I was neck deep in corporate America and construction at the time. The income was tremendous. Despite the wonderful life the world saw, my friend could see me frantically trying to keep my head above water. During the darkest time of my life, my friend stayed with me and helped me stay afloat.

Nicole and I started using the products we now distribute fifteen years before we joined the company. They're what brought my beautiful wife through her storm and helped, our daughter, Savannah survive the waves. So, when Josh joined the corporate side of the company that manufactured the products we'd been blessed to use for nearly fifteen years at that point, it was natural for him to invite me to join the team as a distributor leader in the field. Afterall, he knew me well, believed in me, and knew I had a rockstar wife with a heart the size of Texas, Nicole.

It took eighteen months of genuine care, investing into our relationship and persistence for him to help me realize that I should come on board, and it was another sixteen months before I handed the construction business over to my brother and cousins. But during that time Josh started asking questions—the right questions.

Josh asked me to decide what things in life were most important to me and what I really wanted out of life. He suggested I consider a few things: What would have to happen during my life so that at the end I felt like it was a success? How much impact did I want to have on others? Did I want my impact to be limited to my family or extend far beyond them? Josh helped me dream again. His questions encouraged me to envision the impact I could make if I was brave enough to chart my course through this new career. Josh was already empowering others in a business of life transformation, and he invited me to do the same. He ultimately challenged me to search for God's vision for my life.

I had to do some real soul searching so I could begin to see the qualities of the individual who would live out this vision to make the greatest impact. I asked myself what changes I needed to make to become the kind of person I admire. How would I need to grow as a person to carry out this new vision and what would my ideal day look like? The answer to these questions helped me as I maneuvered through rehab and began to rebuild my life.

I've created a helpful worksheet called The Life Transformer™ that you can use to discover where you currently are, where you want to be, and the actions you need to take to become that person to get you there. You'll find the free download at AllanBlain.com/lhsa or by scanning the following QR Code.

As I began to gain clarity on my vision, I felt like I finally had something strong enough for God to use to keep me on top of the waves. By focusing my sights on my vision, I could look beyond the challenges and keep moving through them with passion, persistence, and hope for a better tomorrow. I grew to realize nothing would stop the turbulent waters, and I determined they weren't going to stop me anymore either.

In order to stay afloat, your why must be bigger than something you can do on your own. If it's too easy, you may get bored and not rely on the Master Builder; too big, and fear might be an anchor dragging you under. God's vision will always be the perfect fit. So when we attempt to draft our own purpose, we miss the excitement and beauty of what God has for us.

True success means you've gained a calling and you're open to that vision growing and changing. Often God shows us only the piece of the puzzle we need for the moment. We may embark on a journey and plan to travel that path the rest of our days. But water-walkers have learned the art of keeping their focus on Jesus. We know that the vision God gave us could very well be the first chapter in an exciting suspense novel.

Because Nicole and I have been living out our vision, after just seven years in our new endeavor, we were honored to be named the number one business in North America for the two-hundred-million-dollar a year company we represent. Even more thrilling for us is to now have several of the top teams in North America within our organization—people we have the honor to work with, mentor, coach and serve. There is nothing more rewarding than seeing those we help win big!

By the grace of God we've been able to use our success to demonstrate to others that success is possible even in the midst of some pretty horrific waves. A lot of people I meet feel like their life challenges–their waves–keep them from achieving like Nicole and I have been able to. It's a recurring theme.

Embracing this life God has called us to has enabled us to share our wave experiences with others. Part of my calling includes telling my story and letting others know that even though the waves keep coming, we can thrive–the primary reason I started the Life's Hard Succeed Anyway podcast in 2022.

We will always find reasons to avoid fulfilling our purpose, but succeeding anyway means having that ark ready and riding out the storms trusting that God promised to work everything for good. (Romans 8:28) Often the good is difficult to see until we've completely cleared that wave and the next one has begun to form, but regardless of where we are in the process, we can succeed because God has uniquely equipped each of us to do so.

With a definitive, God-given purpose, life will have meaning. You won't need to escape or ignore the waves anymore because you'll have a reason to forge ahead.

As you formulate your purpose, you can start to plan the deck. If a dinghy or a canoe was big enough to hold our vision, we could stop with the hull, but we're building an ark because only a massive boat can withstand the storms of life and ride on top of the waves.

## An Ark Needs a Deck

Noah had three decks on his boat. You might have fewer. But an ark-sized vessel without at least one deck would be useless and dangerous. The deck provides stability for the wide hull. It helps hold the boat together and offers a workspace on top of the storage compartment. My life began to change when I started reading God's word, but my vision expanded because Josh challenged me to look outside myself.

On our ark, we build the deck when we begin to look at the way our vision can impact the world. Success is a journey, and as I began to take responsibility for my mistakes, and started looking ahead to what I wanted our future to look like, my vision came alive.

Nicole and I feel compelled to be good stewards of the gifts, talents, abilities, and opportunities God has given us. We see ourselves as part of an enormous mission in the process of blessing many others. By maximizing everything God has blessed us with, we can remain Kingdom focused, allowing us to live the abundant life Jesus talked about.

I remember one of the guests that I interviewed on my *Life's Hard Succeed Anyway* podcast, Joshua Brown, shared that he was born to a fifteen-year-old mother and grew up in a rough part of town. He has since started a pressure washing business that is doing millions in revenue. He calls himself the Pressure Washing Pastor and uses it as a vehicle to minister to others in the community. He is a great example of using one's talents, abilities and business as a mission, just as we are thrilled to be doing with ours.

> I HAVE COME THAT YOU MIGHT HAVE LIFE, AND HAVE IT MORE ABUNDANTLY – JOHN 10:10B

To make the deck strong, we need a cause as big as our vision. My cause began with building myself into the kind of person worthy of my Creator, my wife, my family, and the team I envisioned leading. I started reading more intentionally and gave up things that didn't push me toward my best self. However, self-improvement alone isn't a big enough cause for an ark-sized life. Personal growth and development must be a means to an end—more effectively carrying out the purpose and vision.

After we decide the kind of person we want to become, we have more questions to ask. What is the reason behind your vision? What is the purpose? What cause will your vision support as you navigate the waves?

Noah's cause was saving humanity. If he didn't live out his calling, life on earth would end. My cause is similar. I want to save people from a lot of pain I've experienced by helping them see that life is less about what happens to us and more about how we react to it. My friend Josh helped me see that I wasn't wired to find happiness in more money or a CEO title. I needed my life to have meaning. Josh's questions opened my eyes to see that a big bank account would never bring contentment. The dollars only became significant after I caught the vision and saw how the dollars fit in. Now, every dollar I deposit represents another life being positively impacted. That's a great feeling and a strong motivator.

It was during my darkest days that Nicole and I started our life transformation business, and our lives were the first to be made new. Through the products we offer others and the community God's blessed us with, our cause has developed into a plan to help people in the areas of improved health, added meaning and purpose, and financial solutions. Hopefully, you know yours.

In the process we've become relationally rich beyond our wildest imaginations and have also experienced huge financial blessings from our heavenly Father. However, we want our lives to be so much bigger than a greater income.

## Making it a Houseboat

By adding the deck, we took our ark from a canoe to a deck boat. But we want something that will withstand hurricane strength waves of life—something worthy of a God-size vision.

There's a good chance Noah didn't build the ark alone. His sons, Japheth, Ham, and Shem would have been there to assist him. His father Lamech and grandfather Methuselah both lived to within five years of the flood, too.

We need a community to build our ark as well. Ecclesiastes 4:12 tells us "One person may be easily overpowered, but two can defend themselves. A cord of three strands is not easily broken." We were not meant to live solitary lives. God created us for community. Though few like to admit they need others so badly, the U.S. Surgeon General recently reported "widespread loneliness in the U.S. poses health risks as deadly as smoking up to fifteen cigarettes daily." [9]

During my darkest season, when I appeared to have everything going for me outwardly, I had a hard time facing the fact loneliness and a lack of purpose might be a problem. I had a wonderful family, a loving and supportive wife, and a great crew at work. However, the travel and separation caused me to miss a lot in my children's lives. Despite their love, I often felt like an outsider. My schedule meant I couldn't get involved in mid-week church activities, and while everyone I loved was building community during the week, I was working away from home.

Looking back, in addition to not trusting God and my lack of vision as I battled my hardest storm, I can see that loneliness and lack of community made a big contribution to my darkest season and my attempt to numb it with drinking. I don't want to make it an excuse, but without identifying the problem, it can't be fixed.

So many people deny their need for a meaningful community. They tell themselves they're OK,

9    Seltz, Amanda. *Washington Post.* "Loneliness Poses Health Risks as Deadly as Smoking U.S. Surgeon General Says." May 2, 2023. https://www.pbs.org/newshour/amp/health/loneliness-poses-health-risks-as-deadly-as-smoking-u-s-surgeon-general-says.

but everyone benefits from being a part of a supportive, transformational community of like-minded individuals.

The business Nicole and I started centers around community. So much so that it precipitated our last relocation. We lived in a beautiful part of the world—right in the middle of nowhere between Spokane, Washington and Canada's British Columbia. We had chosen that location for its simplicity and beauty, but our God-given vision called us to build a community bigger than a town of 2,400 that sat an hour from any significant city could provide. We knew that in order to build an ark that would ride out the waves, we needed a place with a solid church, a growth-minded community, and more options for us and our children.

From time to time, I hear people refer to another as, "a self-made millionaire." I don't believe that's a fair statement. First, we need to acknowledge that any success is a blessing from God. Yes, cultivating those blessings means embracing the vision and adding a lot of hustle and hard work, but true success ultimately comes by being able to communicate the vision and surrounding oneself with people willing to invest in that vision with us on some level. Those who have financial success— any success—have a tribe of positive, like-minded individuals who helped lift them to that position, whether they want to acknowledge it or not.

This ark building endeavor is actually a big circle. My friend Josh was adding to his house-boat when he brought me into his community. He helped open my eyes to the vision God had for me and supported me while I slowly added boards to my hull. Now, part of making my ark bigger and better is giving guidance to those who are building their hull and crafting their vision by inviting them into our community.

Nicole and I have learned that a growing com-munity also has several layers, and it's extremely important to be intentional about the people who will be in the layer closest to us. The answer to the following question helps us narrow down who should be our biggest influencers. "Do I want my children to imitate these individuals when they grow up?" If we don't think that person would be a good influence on our beautiful nineteen- and sixteen-year-old daughters, Kaitlin and Peyton, then that person likely wouldn't be a great influ-ence on us either and therefore, isn't a right fit for our inner circle. We use the same criteria for movies, radio stations, books, and more. Inputs matter. The people you surround yourself with make a difference.

We realized years ago that if we wanted to change our lives, we had to change our crowd. We want the people closest to us to inspire us to be our best selves, fan our flame and draw the greatness out of us—something we desire to do for others. On the other hand, we avoid adding folks who constantly talk about people and problems. The Bible has much to say about avoiding these types of people. They do not facilitate successful living.

> GREAT MINDS DISCUSS IDEAS; AVERAGE MINDS DISCUSS EVENTS; SMALL MINDS DISCUSS PEOPLE."
> - ELEANOR ROOSEVELT

Yes, we left some wonderful people on the shores of our past, and we visit them from time to time because we love them. However, we have gained a community that aligns with and supports our aspirations and goals. They love us and bless us and tell us what we need to hear, not just what we want to hear. They celebrate our wins and don't criticize.

Your community will determine the depth of your reach. Every individual you allow into your life on a regular basis influences your thinking. The ripple effect means you will adopt their mindset and pass it on to those you mentor. When you surround yourself with a community that positively affects you, you can more positively affect others.

## Having a Seaworthy Vessel

Successfully riding the waves and surviving the turbulent waters requires developing clarity on your calling, cause, and community. It doesn't happen overnight anymore than you can build a boat in a day. Nevertheless, once I gained clarity on where I was going and my purpose in going there, the picture of who I should be became clear.

To keep a boat seaworthy, it needs regular maintenance. On most cruise lines, you'll find the crew painting or repairing something every time you make port. And once every few years, the huge ship goes into dry dock for a grand overhaul.

Likewise, I continually focus on the qualities, characteristics, and behaviors that I want to see displayed in Allan Blain. I intentionally ask myself what my mindset, attitude, and heart look like in every decision and make adjustments as needed. Am I living like the person I aspire to be?

I embrace the words of Jeremiah 29:11 "For I know the plans I have for you," declares the Lord, "plans to prosper you and not to harm you, plans to give you hope and a future." And I believe God spoke them for each of us. Our Heavenly Father created every person with a purpose and a calling. Jesus didn't sacrifice Himself so we could have a mediocre existence.

God doesn't merely call us out of a sinful, harmful, and damaging life. He calls us into a life of purpose and passion. It's not always easy, but it's certainly an adventurous and rewarding life worth living. We are wired for a passionate and purpose filled life of mission. That's why so many people ask the question, "What am I here for?" When we refuse to embody our calling or live ignorant of the beauty in our purpose, life becomes difficult and frustrating.

Accepting God's vision changes everything.

The clearer my vision became, the more it positively impacted my choice of friends. You've probably heard of the law of association. We all become the people we spend significant time with. It's a general principle that vision attracts. Successful people want to spend time with those who offer a big, positive vision.

Crafting a compelling vision meant that we reimagined our community. We saw ourselves slowly detaching from close associations who didn't add to our vision. We found three types of friends— those whose vision mirrored ours, those whose vision was greater than ours, and those who aspired to have a vision as great as ours. It wasn't that we ditched the people we had known before, but as our priorities shifted, so did the winds that drove our ship. We were armed with tools needed to head into the waves if necessary, while the people with no vision kept getting swept under and didn't want any help to get out.

This process of developing our vision also changed our perspective on time and money. We began to analyze how we spent our time. Why do some people seem to accomplish so much in such a short time and others accomplish so little? We created a list of things that filled up our twenty-four hour days and then asked which of those things served our vision and which did not. Ultimately, we cut out things that didn't contribute to our vision.

For example, we chose to stop watching television, and we eliminated reading or listening to the news. Prior to this, we took a lot of satisfaction in having an immaculate yard and a perfect house. We decided that having a weedless yard didn't put us any closer to our calling. We knew if we wanted to realize the full potential of our vision, we had to make every second count.

Finally, our vision began to dictate our habits. It molded our to-do list. We prioritized reading educational books and becoming lifelong learners and growers. Listening to podcasts became important, and physical fitness moved to the forefront. We stepped into a vision to be an example and an encouragement to others. And in order to promote a high energy, high impact life, we realized we needed to work out, get adequate fluids, eat right, and sleep well.

Our healthy habits also included becoming spiritually mature, not only for ourselves but also so that we could assist others in their faith walk. That meant being very intentional with prayer, meditation, Bible reading, and journaling. Becoming a more Godly father and mother topped our list of priorities, so our habits included a commitment to investing quality time in our children.

We also feel blessed to have a marriage that outperforms most great marriages. That happens because we put each other first, each give one hundred percent, lay down our lives for each other, and don't compromise on our daily time, weekly date nights and quarterly getaways with each other. Only our relationship with our Lord and Savior Jesus Christ comes before our marriage and our children, which serves to strengthen both.

Waves are inevitable, but a Godly vision with a compelling calling, a commendable cause, and a caring community will carry you through.

## Building the Boat

Our boat has seen us through many tragedies. I'm not certain how I might have handled my brother's death after all the other turmoil if we hadn't discovered our vision and begun to build our community. The ark has seen us through the hurt and shame of my youngest sister's poor choices and felony conviction, as well as having to watch our sixteen-year-old son, Braden get mixed up in drugs for a season.

By the time Braden was eighteen it was so bad that we felt it best for him and the rest of our family to ask him to leave the house. Words fail to communicate how extremely difficult this was for us to do. Thankfully, we had the support of numerous friends like Pastor Robby Gallaty who wrote the foreword to this book and others who had overcome addiction. All of them confirmed that enabling him would not be helpful. We knew hitting his rock bottom was the only thing that would create a desire for change. Our son was not in a good place mentally or physically, and he had thrown his cell phone in the river a week prior.

He honored our request and moved out. Within a couple weeks, he found himself homeless, living on the streets of Tampa, Florida, and sleeping in a park in a dangerous part of the city. In the past, I'm not sure we would have had the strength to withstand such a large wave. Nicole and I prayed. Nicole prayed specifically that God would use anyone, even another homeless person, to speak to Braden's heart, and He did just that.

After hearing Braden's story, a homeless man in the park quoted Proverbs 26:11 "As a dog returns to its vomit, so also a fool repeats his foolishness," and asked him, "Why would you rather sleep in a park than your parent's home—even if you have to obey basic rules?"

This pierced his heart, and although he didn't realize that a guy got stabbed very close to where he was sleeping the night before, he borrowed a phone and asked us to come get him.

He'd asked to come back home before, but previously he had not been willing to admit he had a problem, so as difficult as it was for both Nicole and me, we had told him he couldn't come home until he was ready for help.

This time was different though. He agreed to go wherever we wanted to send him. He was broken and ready for change. That likely would not have come so soon had we kept him in our home, enabling him to continue his destructive lifestyle. We sent him to the one year long Adult and Teen

Challenge program. Within a week, he surrendered his life to Christ, and has become a true man of God. We are basking in God's goodness and enjoying having a deep, meaningful relationship with our only son. Nicole and I couldn't be more grateful and proud of him.

I'm thankful I have a success story to share with you about Braden, and Nicole and I pray we'll have a similar one to bring about his older sister, Lacey, one day. But until that time, we praise God for this ark He's given us to weather the storms, and we invite you to build one too.

- **Become An Arkitect™.** While building community seems to finish off our boat, it is also a great place to begin. You'll need a great vision to be an Arkitect™, and one of the best places to start is with a mentor who can ask you the right questions. Surround yourself with people who have big visions, pray about your vision, and listen for God to reveal His plan.
- **Craft the Hull.** Define your why. What do you want your life to look like in ten years? Meet with a mentor or coach who can help you sift through your gifts and talents, your past and your trials, so you can find your

call. It may or may not have anything to do with a career change as it did for me.

- **Build the Deck.** Choose a cause. Who do you want to impact? Where do these people live? Your cause may be as close as next door or as far away as Zimbabwe. When you know who you will serve, it will be easier to decide where you should go.
- **Add the Houseboat.** Build a community. When the waves started crashing over the side, I'm sure Noah was grateful he had a roof on his craft. Your community will be just as powerful. A tribe of like-minded, uplifting, positive peers can encourage us in the direction of our shared mission, values, and objectives. You may even discover your calling and your cause by simply investing time in relationships.
- **Make it Seaworthy.** Never stop growing. Learn from others and learn from your mistakes. Read scripture, gather with small groups. Find books, podcasts, and blogs that focus on your mission and those areas that we talked about in the staging ground. Journaling is another great way to learn and grow.

With a strong staging area and a solid ark you're ready to face the waves head on and seize the life you were created for.

# PART THREE

# RIDING THE WAVES

# CHAPTER SIX

# SEIZING THE LIFE YOU WERE CREATED FOR

In July 2018, Eloy Lorenzo, a Brazilian surfer, found the perfect wave in Uluwatu, Bali. Some have claimed it's the longest ride ever caught on camera, and people who watched it scored it at 9.37. No one can estimate how fast Lorenzo was going; however, the video shows him severely out pacing the Jet Ski that followed him on the backside of the wave. For seventy-two seconds Lorenzo stayed just ahead of the crash. He had complete command of the curl, skirting from the trough to the lip in perfect harmony with the water. One YouTube follower compared him to a musician keeping time with the orchestra. [10]

---

[10]  Surfers of Bali. *YouTube.*"Longest Wave Ever Filmed at Uluwatu. https://www.youtube.com/watch?v=U1Ih2HN463s&t=74s

Professional surfers only dream about that kind of wave. Research shows that the average surfer only spends three minutes out of every twenty actually riding waves, and if they can catch one for a full minute, it's considered rare. [11]

Sadly, most people assume the waves of life don't give them any better odds.

During the second act of Finding Nemo, a distressed Marlin tells Dorie, "I promised I'd never let anything happen to him." A confused Dorie replies, "That's a funny thing to promise." Of course, Marlin doesn't understand, so Dorie explains. "Well, you can't never let anything happen to him. Then nothing would ever happen to him."

While it sounds good at face value, a wave-free life would be just as dissatisfying as the life Marlin tried to provide Nemo. We will have waves. But now you have the blueprint to building a boat to withstand the storms and ride out the swells.

Life is hard. Never minimize that fact. But you now have the tools to build a boat that can withstand any storm. Regardless of the level of difficulty, you can succeed anyway.

---

[11]    *Surfer Today.* Accessed June 20, 2023/ https://www.surfertoday.com/surfing/surfers-only-spend-8-of-the-time-riding-waves.

## Going All In

Embracing your vision will give you a clarity like you've never known before. Though it didn't happen overnight, when Nicole and I reached that place where our vision became our passion, it was as if we stepped out of the stormy fog into a cloudless day. The seas were open in front of us, the compass and soundings were clear, and we had a structure that would ride out the waves. Our vision gave us purpose and a mission. It is our navigational device, and it drives our lifestyle.

But in order to really enjoy the boat ride, we had to leave the dock. Going all in means leaving things behind that cause detours or get in the way of fulfilling your vision.

I wish someone had taught me the principle of association when I was a youth, though I'm not certain I would have understood it or heeded the advice.

We are the average of the five people we spend the most time with. Dan Pena put it like this, "Show me your friends, and I'll show you your future."

> SHOW ME YOUR FRIENDS, AND I'LL SHOW YOU YOUR FUTURE.
> ~ DAN PENA

1 Corinthians 5:3 tells us "Bad company corrupts good character."

Unfortunately, not everyone will rejoice in our success. Even though we invite them to join us on our boat and offer to help them build their own, some will still choose the dinghy lifestyle. And that's okay. But some are more like crabs in a bucket.

Did you know that if you put one crab in a bucket, it can get out? But if you put several crabs in that same bucket, they'll be stuck there. When one tries to claw his way up, the others will pull him back. I don't know if they don't like being left alone, they're jealous of their fellow crab, or they're afraid of what lies outside the bucket. Whatever their motivation, they can't watch the other crab succeed ahead of them.

It's important to understand that an entire sea of water can't sink a ship unless it gets inside the ship. Likewise, the unsuccessful mindsets of others can't pull you down unless you allow it to get inside you. This can unknowingly happen over time when spending too much time around negative, narrow minded, fixed mindset people. We may have to leave behind the old associations with people who pull us down in order to live the successful life we are called to live.

Nicole and I picked up and moved halfway across the country to increase the population we could impact as we continued to expand our new tribe. However, it meant leaving everything comfortable.

> THE ONE WHO WALKS WITH WISE WILL BECOME WISE, BUT A COMPANION OF FOOLS WILL SUFFER HARM.
> - PROVERBS 13:20

I knew the construction business, and the money couldn't have been better. Still, that comfortable place was mediocre compared to the vision God had for us. Boarding the ark meant a significant cut in income at the time. Plus, I handed over my ownership of the multi-million dollar construction company with no compensation in return. God invited me to be like Abraham and move to a "land I will show you." (Genesis 12:1) Going all in isn't easy, but it helped catapult me to a new level in my faith journey and my life adventure, and we've never regretted a moment of everything we gave up.

Familiar and comfortable anchor themselves in complacency. We think we're happy until we wake up one day and discover we've settled. God's vision may make you extremely uncomfortable, but there's nothing quite so exciting as the adventure of leaving comfortable on the shore.

# Stay Motivated and Learn to Fail

Even with a clear vision and a passion for your cause, we have days when we struggle to get motivated. But just because it happens to everyone doesn't mean we can use that as an excuse to lose momentum. The key is to take action even when you don't feel like it.

Your brain is wired to keep you alive and minimize risks. So when something we know we should do makes us uncomfortable, we need to act quickly before our brain can process the information and try to talk us out of doing things that aren't easy.

It would be wonderful if everything we needed to do to carry out our vision was easy, fun, and comfortable. But let's face it, only those who practice hours every day become world class musicians. Champion athletes practice six days a week for their three hours on the field. You will have days when you don't feel like doing what you know you need to do. People who succeed anyway are driven by their vision not their feelings. Our choices and actions directly impact our outcomes. So we have to enter each day with an "I will" attitude.

Another thing that interferes with our motivation is fear. Fear of failing, fear of what others will think, and fear of repercussions are just a few of the things that stop us when we need to be following our vision.

Nicole's favorite quote is "Everything you want is on the

> EVERYTHING YOU WANT IS ON THE OTHER SIDE OF FEAR.
> - JACK CANFIELD

other side of fear." It reminds her that fear is merely an obstacle, something to be conquered. Did you know that studies have shown that over ninety percent of the things we fear never happen,[12] and many times the things that look scary help us grow, bring excitement, or make us laugh when we reach the other side?

The fear of failure in particular just means we haven't practiced enough yet. Think about a child learning to walk. They hold onto the couch because they fear falling. By the time they're five they won't even hold on when you ask them to because they've done it successfully so many times the fear is gone. It may help to remember courage is a muscle, and the more you work it the

---

[12]   Heid, Markham, *Elemental,* August 15, 2019 "Most Things You Worry About Will Never Actually Happen." https://elemental.medium. com/most-things-you-worry-about-will-never-actually-happen-83bff850c5f9#.

stronger it will become. You'll still have fear, but your courage will be big enough to tackle it.

Maybe we need to consider that when we don't try, we've failed already. Failure helps us grow. In fact, the more mistakes you make, the faster you learn. Those who succeed have discovered one of their most powerful tools is to fail fast.

I love the story of Sarah Blakely, Spanx creator and the world's youngest female "self-made" billionaire. When she was a child, her father would excitedly ask how she had failed that day. If she and her brother had no answer, her father would be disappointed. On the other hand, their best shortcomings earned them high-fives and accolades. She said her dad reframed failure. To her failure meant not trying new things. [13]

> SUCCESS CONSISTS OF GOING FROM FAILURE TO FAILURE WITHOUT THE LOSS OF ENTHUSIASM.
> - WINSTON CHURCHILL

If you adopt Sarah Blakely's mindset, you can't fail if you make an honest attempt. The lack of motivation, fear, and that sense of failure all begin in our

---

[13] *Noteworthy Nonsense. "Reframing Failure: What Did You Fail at Today?"* Accessed July 6, 2023. https://noteworthynonsense.com/blog/08/2020/Blakely-Failure

minds. When we daily decide to act even when it's uncomfortable, we don't feel like it, or we're afraid, we transform our brain. Little by little, our changed mindset gives us freedom, power, and the opportunity to seize life and become all we are created to be.

It's not possible to exercise faith and fear at the same time because faith takes our focus off the fear. Likewise, focusing on our long range goals and where our vision is taking us helps us avoid staring at our immediate problems. Instead of obsessing over mistakes, being brought down by obstacles, and allowing difficulties to take our attention away from our next positive action step, we can use the direction our vision provides to move through the situation effectively.

We must be intentional to make our success story larger than our excuse story. When our vision of a better future is bigger than our excuses, no challenge can stop us.

## Get a Mentor, Be a Mentor

Ever since Nicole and I grabbed hold of our vision, we have placed ourselves in circles with whole-life mentors as well as role mentors. Whole-life mentors are a rare breed. They have achieved success in every area of life where we aspire to succeed. They aren't perfect, but they've found the fruit of the Spirit in ways that few do. These folks have learned to balance their health, marriage, family, free time, business, and finances. We praise God for putting them into our lives, and we watch how they live so we can imitate the Christ-like behaviors that catapulted them to success. Do you have one or more whole-life mentors in your life? If not, I highly encourage you to seek one out.

Role mentors, as my dear friend and business partner Chad Johnson referred to them on Episode 18 of my *Life's Hard Succeed Anyway* podcast, also help us achieve results. These folks have exceptional success in one particular area. We don't want to imitate them in every aspect, but we know that they can give us guidance in the areas they excel in. For example, a physical fitness and health mentor may not live in such a manner that I want them to influence me spiritually, relationally, or professionally, as an example.

It's important to understand the difference between whole-life and role mentors because if we aren't intentional, we might sub-consciously model the unhealthy areas of the role mentor's life. Those less than successful areas don't mean we shouldn't look to them for guidance in their area of expertise and strength; however, we need to be aware so we can keep ourselves on the right track.

We appreciate the accountability these beautiful people give us. We follow them and give them permission to point out trouble spots in their niche areas. We count on them to notice when we get out of alignment.

If you look at your tribe, you'll find people who inspire you–people whose lives give you hope and help you see the goals you aspire to reach are possible. I encourage you to reach out to these folks, take them to dinner, look for ways to serve them and add value to their lives, ask questions, and listen to their stories. You'll find that even though it looks like everything is smooth sailing now, they have weathered unimaginable storms. I've never met anyone with any measure of success who has had an easy life–only those who have made a decision to succeed even though life is hard. Those are the people you want to look to as mentors. Learn life's lessons from them.

One of the most rewarding parts of carrying out our vision is growing to the point that we can help mentor those who are new to the ark building business. We've been blessed to build a large tribe in our life transformation enterprise. Sharing our story, our failures and successes, allows others to grow too.

As you live out your vision, be sure to act in such a way that those around you can learn from you. Even if you feel like you have only one area of life with success, you can be the one who inspires and fans the flame. One of the most exciting parts of seizing life is bringing others along with you.

# CHAPTER SEVEN
# LIFE CAN BE A BEACH

What if life can be a beach? Or a mountainside cabin or a resort on the French Riviera? Whatever you consider idyllic can be the imagery for your life. The secret is in understanding the waves.

For many years Nicole and I looked for success in a wave-free life. Accepting the fact that version of living didn't exist and moving into the understanding that our Heavenly Father had a God-sized vision for us changed everything. Even without the perfection we sought so diligently, we feel as though we landed on our own private sun-filled beach. And we invite you to experience it with us.

Nicole and I tell our story because we want people to see that success is achievable even while the storms crash all around. People who wait for the perfect weather and the ideal wave never leave the beach. They settle for a blanket in the sand or a poolside lounge and get stuck there. Through rain, sun, cold, and storms, they watch life pass them by and act as spectators while they watch others live their dreams and mediocrity steals any bit of hope for beauty and adventure from theirs.

You were created for more than a subpar existence. I want to help you craft your vision, embrace your calling, find your cause, and build your community so you can rise high on the swell, ride the waves of success, and as my good friend Aaron Walker says, live a life of significance.

## Build an Ark

Every week, I share bits of my life and invite others who have learned to rise high on the waves to join me on my podcast, "Life's Hard Succeed Anyway." Look for it on your favorite podcast app–Apple, Spotify, Audible, YouTube, and many others. Nicole and I, as well as our guests, want you to learn from our mistakes and find inspiration in the way God has used even our most trying times to lift us out of the turbulent waters.

Additionally, you'll find links to my *Wisdom Wednesday* weekly emails to help you live a high performance life as well as my *21 Strategies for Ultra Success Living at AllanBlain.com (or you can scan the QR Code above).* And if you'd like to receive the Arkitect Template™ to help you become the Arkitect™ of your own "Ark" download that at Allan-Blain.com/lhsa or (or you can scan the QR Code below).

Nicole and I feel blessed to have found our place and purpose in this world, and nothing brings us more joy than seeing others discover their unique vision so they can conquer the waves.

Success is a journey not a destination. Making progress towards your potential by walking out the purpose and plan God created you for is the ulti-mate success!

## Join Our Community

My wife and I both love to share our message with others. We look forward to coming into your community to share the secret to succeeding in the midst of life's storms. So, if you need a keynote speaker or podcast guest, be sure to reach out. Additionally, we're constantly finding new ways to help people build their ark to enjoy greater impact and increased success through coaching, speaking, masterminds, retreats, and other events. I hope you'll stop by our website at AllanBlain.com to see what we're up to (or scan the following QR Code).

Nicole and I want to work with you. We want to help you find your calling and craft your vision. Our dear friend Josh brought us into a bigger community and inspired us to live out our full potential, and we love doing that for others. We want to inspire you and catapult you to the life of your dreams.

# Find Your Beach

When a person learns to water ski as I grew up doing at Kaweah Lake in Central California, the most important instruction is this, "When you fall, let go of the rope." The instructor will repeat it several times before they start the engine and begin to drag the novice. Still, the first time the new skier falls, he or she will hold on for a short time. It's the natural response when you hit the water.

If you've ever skied, you may already be smiling. If not, you'd never suspect that holding on means the skier goes deeper and deeper under the water. Only by letting go can the person breathe again.

Making changes to live out your vision and letting go of the things that pull us under can be very difficult. It definitely doesn't happen as fast as we'd like. But like holding onto that ski rope, it's even harder to stay the same.

You can settle or succeed, but you can't do both. Settling embraces excuses, success sees obstacles as opportunities. If you're stuck in your perceived limitations, you may need to find a great community that can be a catalyst to assist you in finding your calling or cause. Surround yourself with people who speak positivity into your life and discourage your negative talk and watch your life change.

If you never get rid of the old, you may never find the new. It reminds me of the life of a lobster. Did you know that a lobster's shell doesn't grow with him? His mushy body grows and grows until his shell becomes very uncomfortable. I suppose the crustacean could just settle to live in the pain of a tight shell, but lobsters know that they can't grow or get a new outer layer until they get rid of the old. So, he will crawl under a rock formation to avoid predatory fish and discard that tight shell. As soon as he casts off the old shell a new one grows, and before you know it, he can come out from under the rock. He'll have to repeat the process many times in his life, but each time he'll come out bigger and better than before.

Human life is more like a lobster's than we'd like to admit. When we live without purpose, we feel life's stress and strain, and nothing can change until we make the decision to cast off the old and stop settling. By getting rid of the pain of the old shell, you'll be in a much greater position to find your unique calling. And that will open the door to crafting a compelling vision. You'll find a beautiful cause, and you can begin to attract other like minded individuals to your community; a group of mentors and mentees, friends and colleagues–a variety of individuals who can help you rise above the waves and ride the crest to succeed in the areas most important to you. For me, those things are spiritual success, relational success, physical success, and financial success. All important, but in that order of priority.

I desire to live an exhilarating life–one of growth, not stagnation, a life of passion and excitement. I want to live a life of service to others, not self absorption; of freedom, not dependence; of opportunity, not boundaries; of fulfillment, not dissatisfaction; of abundance, not scarcity. I yearn for a life of meaningful purpose that makes the maximum impact in other's lives, and I am so grateful to now be living that.

Where would you like to see yourself in ten years? How about five years? Next year? What will your life look like ten years from now if nothing changes? Will you be satisfied to remain where you are right now? If not, what short term sacrifices are you willing to make today for your better tomorrow? You weren't created to live a haphazard existence, but rather a life of intentional purpose.

If I can help you in any way please reach out. We invite you to join our free transformational online *Succeed Anyway Community* and check out many of the other free resources I have provided on my website at AllanBlain.com. If you need coaching or a speaker at your next event, we can discuss that too.

You can succeed, and I'd love to help you. By becoming an Arkitect™ and building an ark that can withstand the storms and the waves, you can seize the life you were created for. You may find your dream morphing as you grow, but that just makes the ride more exciting. God has abundance for you. It may or may not be in the form of extreme wealth, but certainly with a life filled with contentment through your storms, security and richness in your relationships, and an unpredictable but deeply meaningful future and a vision bigger than you could ever imagine on your own. (For FREE Resources see pages 151-155).

# A WORD TO THE READER

All profits from the sale of this book will go to support the Adult & Teen Challenge Recovery Ministry. I wrote this book not for profits, but to bless and encourage others. If this book has benefited you in any way, I'd appreciate hearing from you. Would you consider either tagging me in a social media post (I'd love to repost) or simply emailing me what this book meant to you at allan@allanblain.com. Thank you and may God tremendously bless your continued journey as you succeed anyway.

# MEET ALLAN BLAIN

 Allan Blain and his bride of more than thirty years, Nicole, turned a seventy-five dollar investment in 2015 into a six-figure passive income by 2016, which has grown exponentially since. Allan knows how to help everyday people like himself create passive income streams from anywhere without interfering with their primary careers.

Today, they have grown their organization to include over 10,000 others spanning ten countries, producing millions in annual revenue, and representing countless lives that have been positively impacted by both his company's food-based supplements as well as his online business coaching.

Allan thoroughly loves encouraging and inspiring other entrepreneurs by sharing past struggles and mistakes he's overcome, and the mindset and strategies used to massively succeed both in business and at home.

Host of the top ranked podcast "Life's Hard Succeed Anyway," Allan welcomes weekly guests who share stories, struggles and strategies they used to overcome adversity and succeed anyway!

When he's not working, Allan can be found hanging out with his wife and six children at their Nashville lake home, taking others wake-surfing or fishing, training for a triathlon, or dating Nicole.

# SUCCEED ANYWAY

*Join Our Community*

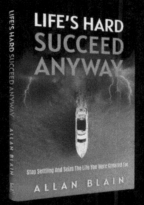

## Maximizing Your Ability to Live a Life of Success in Your Faith, Family, Fitness, and Finances.

### Scan the QR code to link to an email request to join our online community.

# ELEVATE YOUR LIFE

Scan the QR code to link to an email request for more information about our whole-food nutritional supplements and/or the associated income opportunity of partnering with us.

# CONNECT WITH ALLAN

Follow him on your favorite
social media platforms today.

# AllanBlain.com/Contact

# THIS BOOK IS PROTECTED INTELLECTUAL PROPERTY

The author of this book values Intellectual Property. The book you just read is protected by Easy IP™, a proprietary process, which integrates blockchain technology giving Intellectual Property "Global Protection." By creating a "Time-Stamped" smart contract that can never be tampered with or changed, we establish "First Use" that tracks back to the author.

Easy IP™ functions much like a Pre-Patent™ since it provides an immutable "First Use" of the Intellectual Property. This is achieved through our proprietary process of leveraging blockchain technology and smart contracts. As a result, proving "First Use" is simple through a global and verifiable smart contract. By protecting intellectual property with blockchain technology and smart contracts, we establish a "First to File" event.

Powered By Easy IP™

# LEARN MORE AT EASYIP.TODAY

Printed in the USA
CPSIA information can be obtained
at www.ICGtesting.com
CBHW071710260324
5822CB00005B/24

9 781636 802008